INSTANT GUITAR!

FAKEBOOK

with tablature and photo chords

The fakebook designed especially for guitarists.
Play over 150 favorite songs right away.

W9-CND-023

Amsco Publications
New York/London/Paris/Sydney/Copenhagen/Berlin/Tokyo/Madrid

Cover photography by Randall Wallace
Project editor: Peter Pickow
Interior design and layout: Amy Appleby
Editorial assistant: Elaine Adam

Order No. AM 978417
US International Standard Book Number: 0.8256.2795.8
UK International Standard Book Number: 1.84449.224.9

Exclusive Distributors:
Music Sales Corporation
257 Park Avenue South, New York, NY 10010 USA
Music Sales Limited
8/9 Frith Street, London W1D 3JB England
Music Sales Pty. Limited
120 Rothschild Street, Rosebery, Sydney, NSW 2018, Australia

Printed in the United States of America by
Vicks Lithograph and Printing Corporation

Instant Guitar Fakebook

Getting Started

Welcome to the world's easiest songbook for guitarists. Whether you play acoustic or electric guitar, this huge collection will bring you hours of playing pleasure.

All of the songs in this book feature easy-to-read photo chords. These help you to instantly play hundreds of new songs on your own. That's because photo chords show you the exact hand position for each chord before you play it.

All of the tunes feature guitar tablature as well as standard music notation. This lets you play new melodies right away, even if you don't read music.

Beginners and professionals love to use *Instant Guitar Fakebook.* That's because it makes it so easy to play new songs at a glance with confidence and style.

Tuning Your Guitar

You should always take a minute to tune up before you play. This is especially true if you are playing with other musicians. Here are the pitches for each string of the guitar in standard tuning.

STRING	6	5	4	3	2	1
NOTE	E	A	D	G	B	E

The most common tuning method is called *relative tuning*.

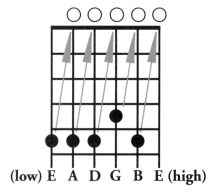

(low) E A D G B E (high)

- Press down on the sixth string (low E) just to the left of the fifth fret, then pluck this string with your other hand to play an A note. Compare this with the A note played on the open fifth string.

- If the fifth string does not sound in tune, use the tuning peg to loosen it until it sounds lower than the sixth string, fifth fret, then slowly bring it up to pitch.

- When your A string is in tune, fret it at the fifth fret. This note is D, and should sound the same as the open D (fourth string).

- When your D string is in tune, fret it at the fifth fret. This note is G, and should sound the same as the open G (third string).

- When your G string is in tune, fret it at the fourth fret. This note is B, and should sound the same as the open B (second string).

- When your B string is in tune, fret it at the fifth fret. This note is E, and should sound the same as the open high E (first string).

Reading Chords

A *chord* is a group of three or more notes that are played together. The pattern of chords in a song is its *chord progression* or *harmony*. Once you know a few chords, you can strum many new songs on your own. You can then sing the melody—or accompany another singer or instrumentalist.

A *chord diagram* is like a snapshot of the guitar neck (held vertically). It shows you where to put your left-hand fingers on the strings, and which strings to play. (If you play a left-handed gutar, you'll use your right hand to fret the strings.)

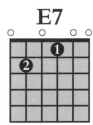

Take a look at the chord diagram for **E7**.

○ The chord name is shown at the top.

○ A number marks each finger's position on the strings.

○ An **o** indicates an *open* string. Play this string without fretting.

○ An **x** indicates a string that you should not play (as shown in the **A+7** and **Fm6** diagrams below).

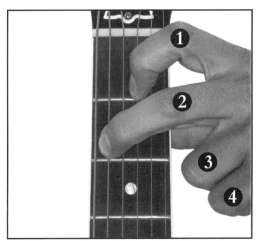

The photo chords in this book are presented horizontally to show the guitar neck in a natural playing position. Because they are so easy to read, photo chords help you to instantly play a wide range of new songs.

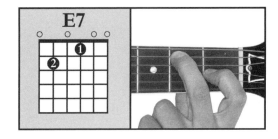

Some chords are played further up the neck of the guitar. In this diagram of the **A+7** chord the Roman numeral V indicates the fifth fret.

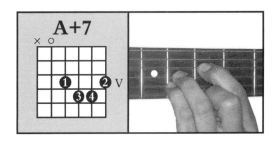

This diagram of the **Fm6** chord features a curved line at the top. This means you should fret three strings with the side of your first finger. This is called *barring*. Because it calls for this technique, the **Fm6** chord is called a *bar chord*.

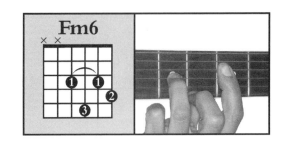

Reading Tablature

Music for the guitar is frequently written in *tablature*. The tablature *staff* is composed of six lines. Each line represents a string of the guitar

- The top line represents the highest string (High E).
- The bottom line represents the lowest string (Low E).

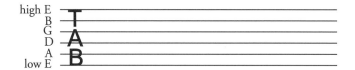

The melody of each song in this book is provided in guitar tablature, as well as standard music notation. Take a look at the first line of "Chicago" in this format.

Numbers on the lines of the tablature staff tell you which frets to play.

- The numeral 0 indicates an unfretted, or open, string.
- The numeral 1 indicates the fret nearest to the tuning pegs.
- The numeral 2 indicates the next highest fret, and so on.

Notes and rests on the music staff show you the rhythm of the melody.

A curved line linking two notes of the same pitch is called a *tie*. When you see this symbol, just hold that pitch for the combined length of both notes. The durations of common notes and rests are shown in the table that follows.

Notes and Rests

Whole Note

Whole Rest

Dotted Half Note

Dotted Half Rest

Half Note

Half Rest

Quarter Note

Quarter Rest

Eighth Note

Eighth Rest

Sixteenth Note

Sixteenth Rest

A dot extends a given note by half its value, thus:

- A half note lasts for two beats, so a dotted half note lasts for three beats.

- A quarter note lasts for one beat, so a dotted quarter note lasts for one-and-a-half beats.

- An eighth note lasts for one-half beat, so a dotted eighth lasts for three-quarters of a beat.

AFTER YOU'VE GONE

Words and music by Henry Creamer & Turner Layton

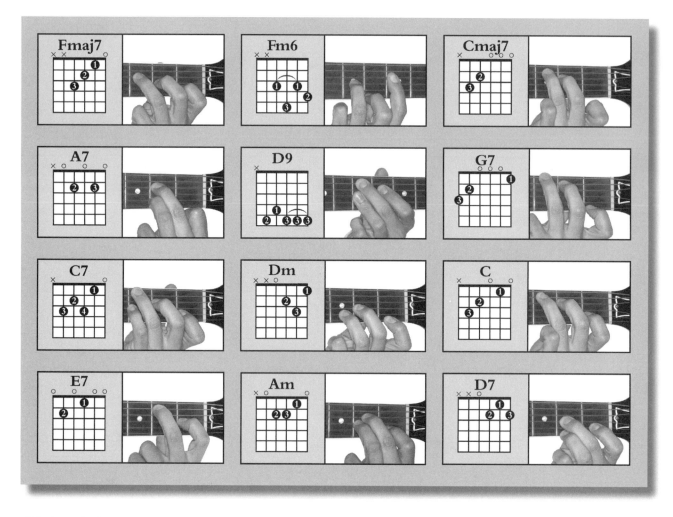

Moderately fast

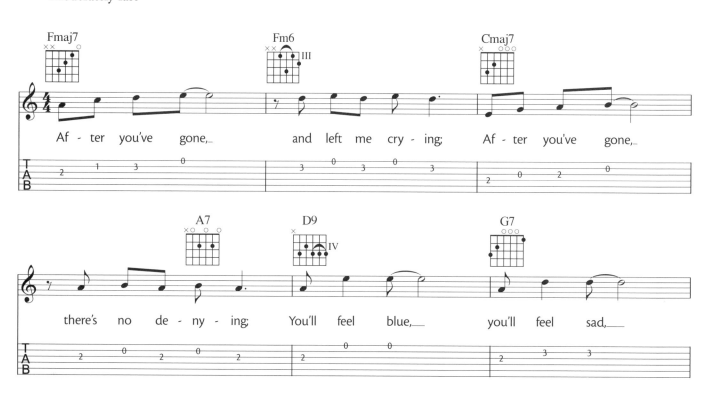

AIN'T WE GOT FUN

Words and music by Richard A. Whiting, Gus Kahn & Raymond B. Egan

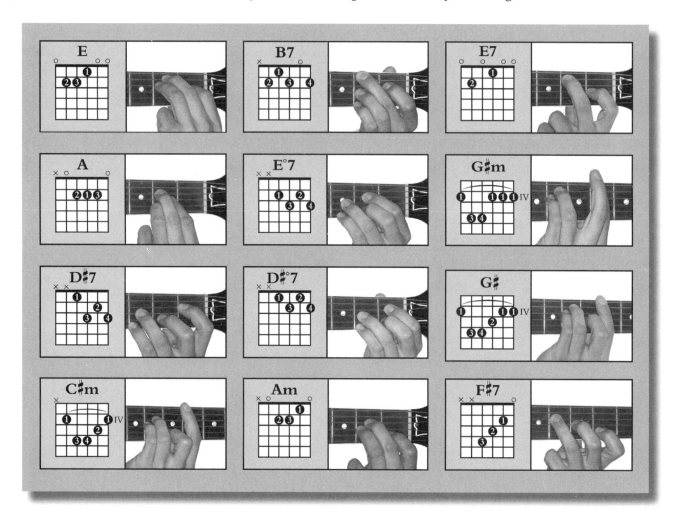

Moderately

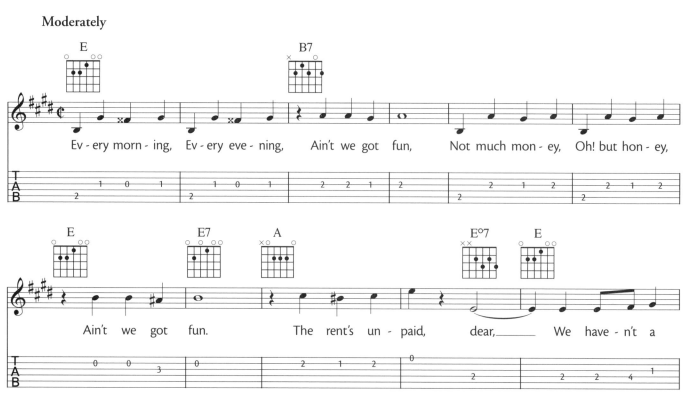

Ev - ery morn - ing, Ev - ery eve - ning, Ain't we got fun, Not much mon - ey, Oh! but hon - ey,

Ain't we got fun. The rent's un - paid, dear,_____ We have - n't a

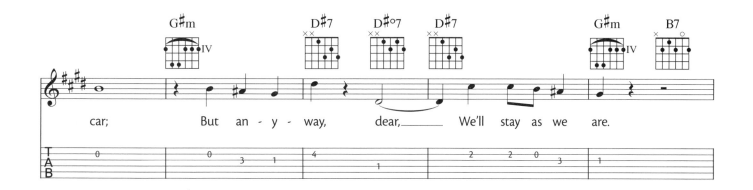

car; But an - y - way, dear,_____ We'll stay as we are.

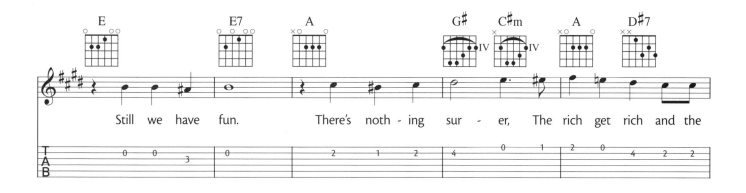

E - ven if we owe the gro - cer, Ain't we got fun, Tax col - lec - tor's get - ting clos - er,

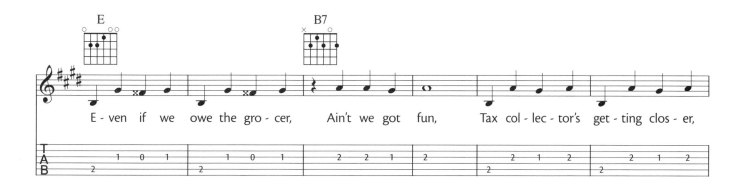

Still we have fun. There's noth - ing sur - er, The rich get rich and the

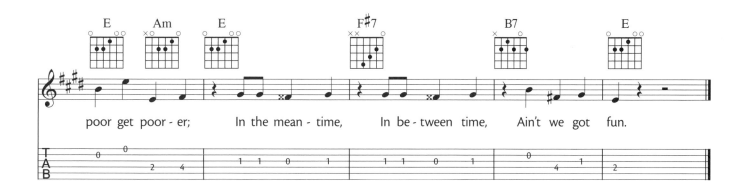

poor get poor - er; In the mean - time, In be - tween time, Ain't we got fun.

ALEXANDER'S RAGTIME BAND

Words and music by Irving Berlin

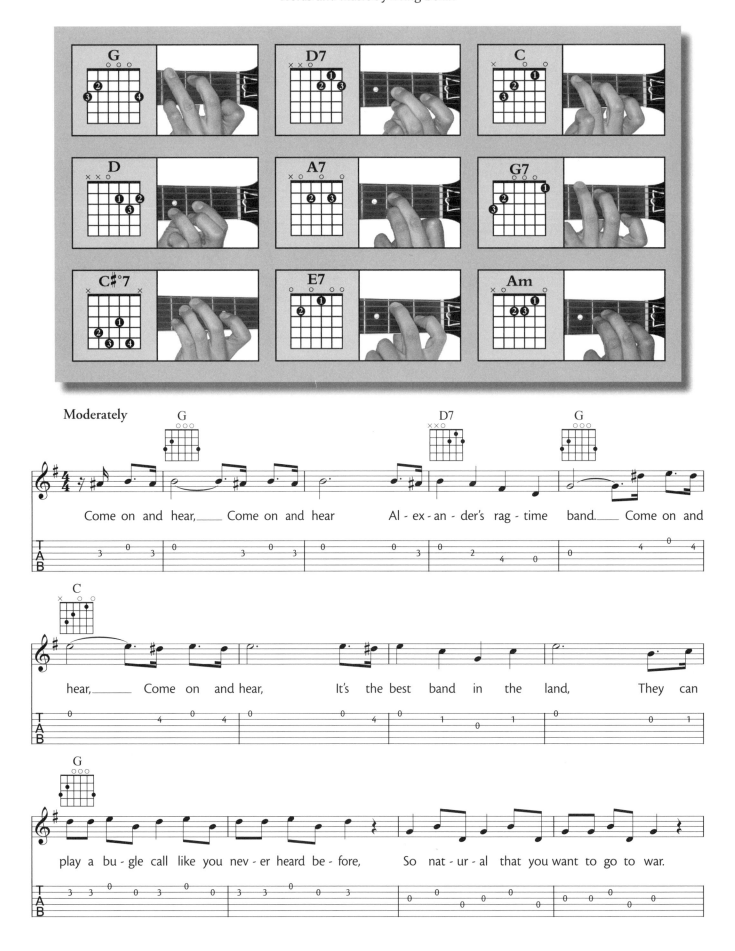

ALICE BLUE GOWN

Words by Joseph McCarthy • Music by Harry Tierney

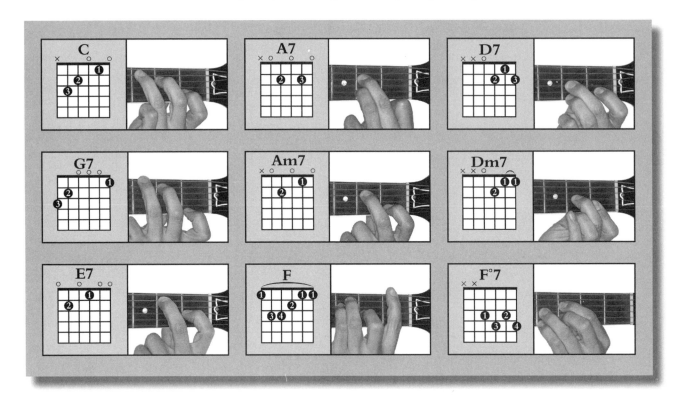

Moderately

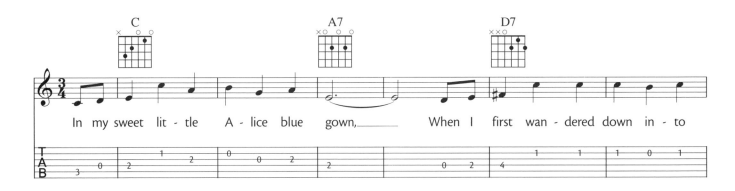

In my sweet lit - tle A - lice blue gown,____ When I first wan - dered down in - to

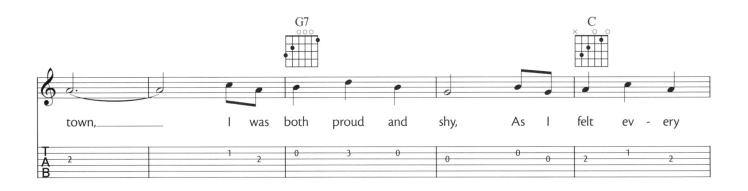

town,____ I was both proud and shy, As I felt ev - ery

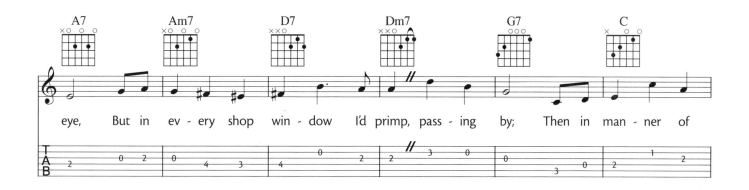

eye, But in ev - ery shop win - dow I'd primp, pass - ing by; Then in man - ner of

fash - ion I'd frown,_____ And the world seemed to smile all a -

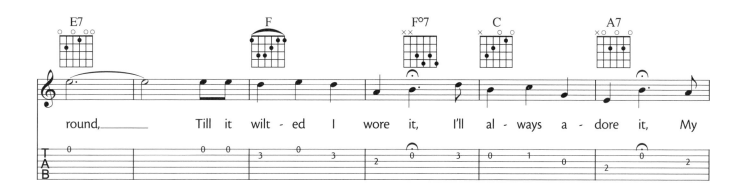

round,_____ Till it wilt - ed I wore it, I'll al - ways a - dore it, My

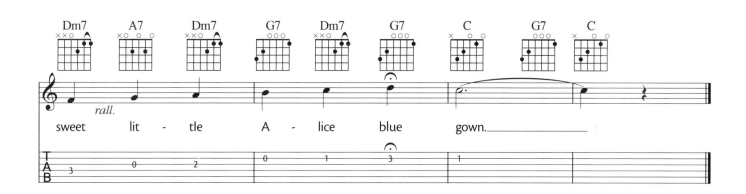

sweet lit - tle A - lice blue gown._____

ALL BY MYSELF

Words and music by Irving Berlin

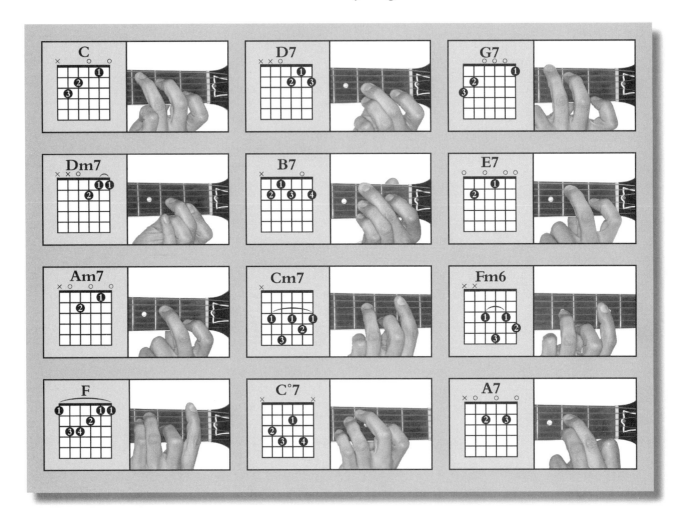

Moderately

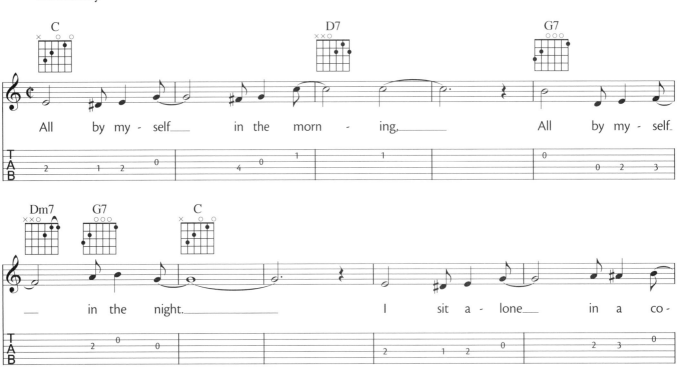

ALOHA OE

Words and music by Queen Liliuokalani

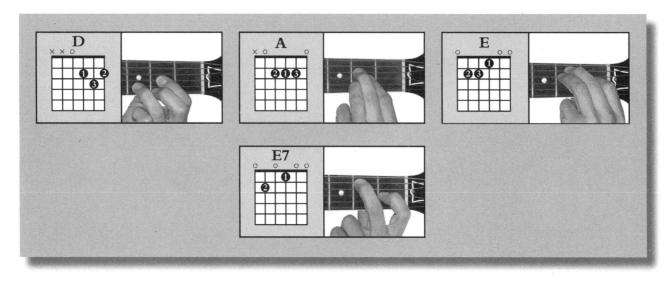

Freely

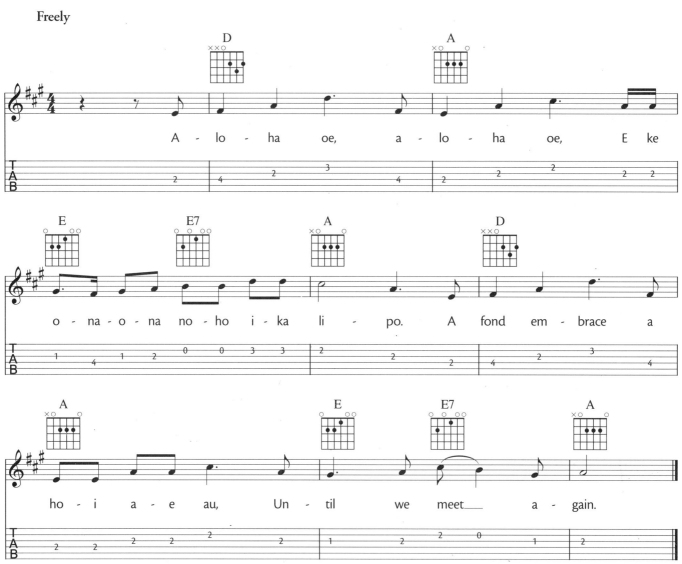

A - lo - ha oe, a - lo - ha oe, E ke

o - na - o - na no - ho i - ka li - po. A fond em - brace a

ho - i a - e au, Un - til we meet___ a - gain.

Farewell to thee, farewell to thee,
Thou charming one who dwells among the bowers.
A fond embrace before I now depart,
Until we meet again.

AMAZING GRACE

Words by John Newton • Music traditional

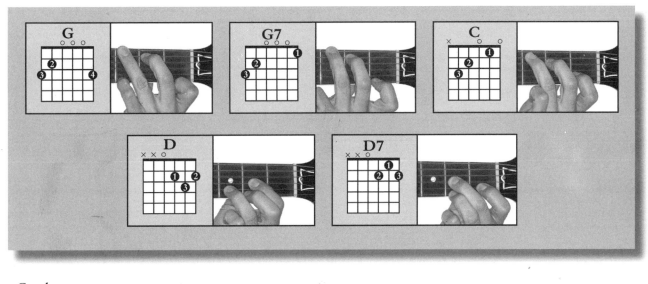

Gently

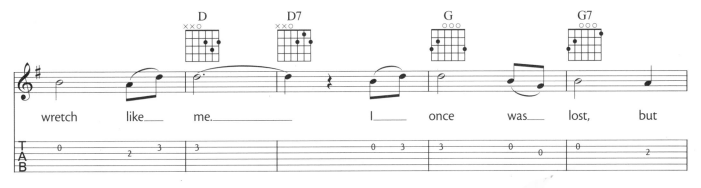

A - maz - ing grace, how sweet the sound That saved a

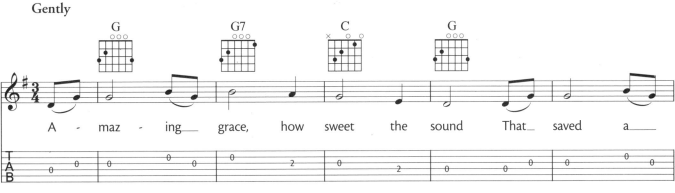

wretch like me. I once was lost, but

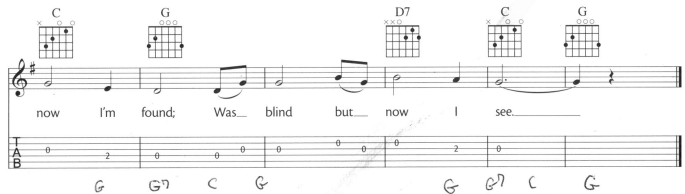

now I'm found; Was blind but now I see.

2. 'Twas grace that taught my heart to fear,
And grace my fears relieved.
How precious did that grace appear
The hour I first believed.

3. Through many dangers, toils, and snares,
I have already come,
'Tis grace that brought me safe thus far,
And grace will lead me home.

AMERICA, THE BEAUTIFUL

Words by Katherine Lee Bates • Music by Samuel Augustus Ward

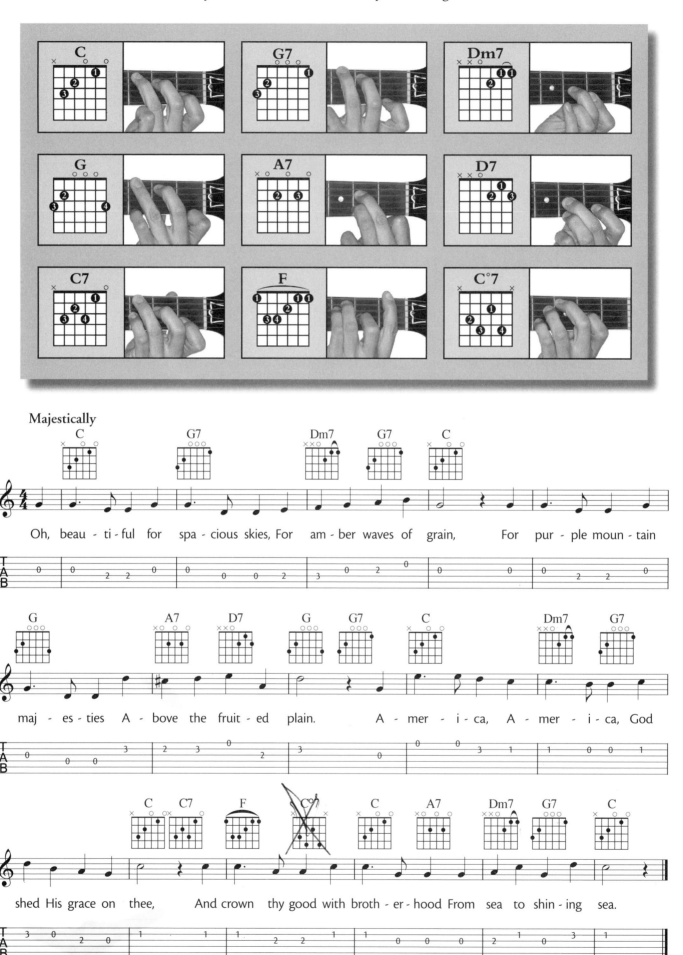

Majestically

Oh, beau - ti - ful for spa - cious skies, For am - ber waves of grain, For pur - ple moun - tain

maj - es - ties A - bove the fruit - ed plain. A - mer - i - ca, A - mer - i - ca, God

shed His grace on thee, And crown thy good with broth - er - hood From sea to shin - ing sea.

ANCHORS AWEIGH

Words by Alfred Hart Miles & R. Lovell • Music by Charles A. Zimmerman

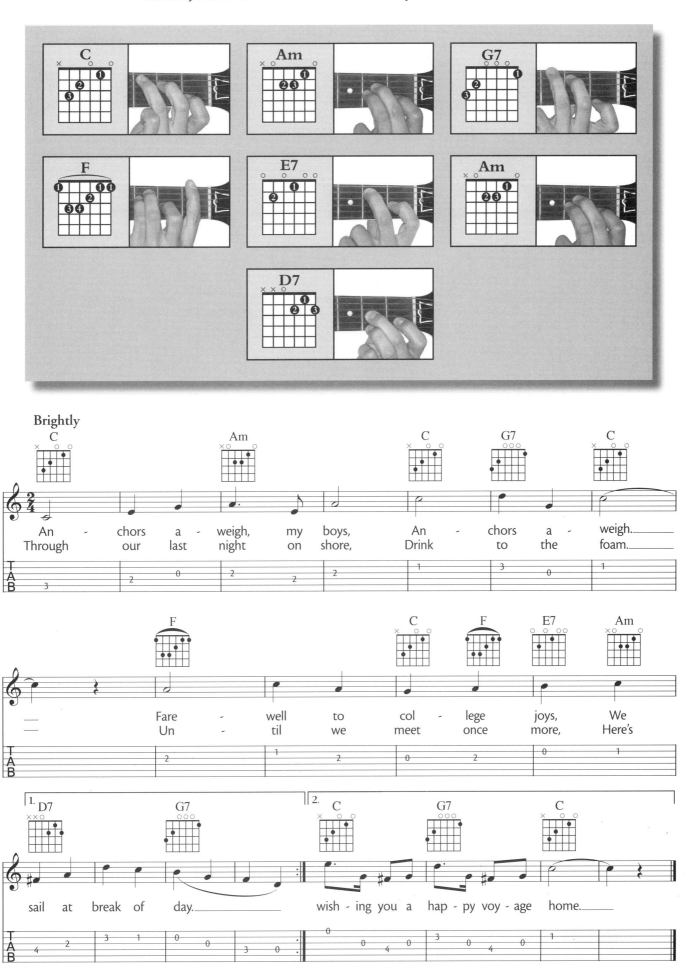

APRIL SHOWERS

Words by B.G. Deslyva • Music by Louis Silvers

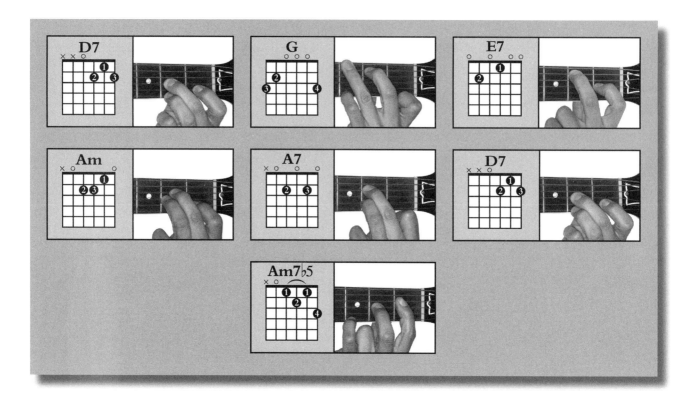

Moderately

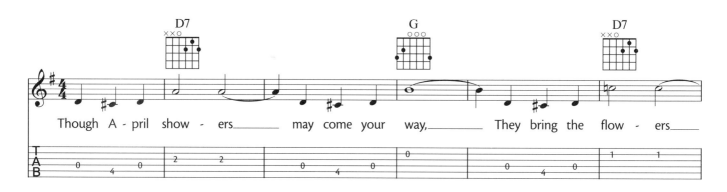

Though A - pril show - ers_____ may come your way,_____ They bring the flow - ers_____

_____ that bloom in May._____ So if it's rain - ing,_____ have no re - grets,_____

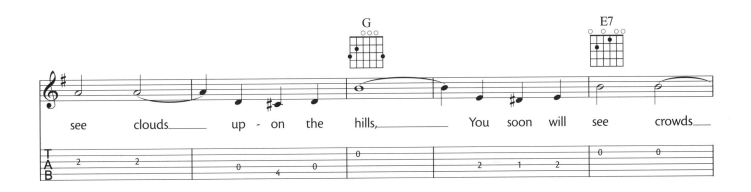

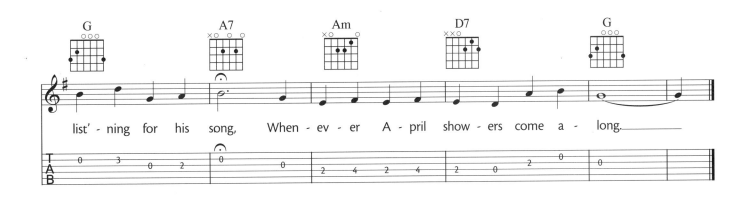

A-TISKET A-TASKET

American folk song

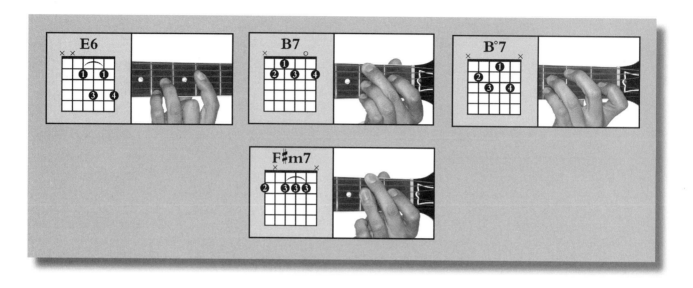

AURA LEE

Words by W.W. Fosdick • Music by George R. Poulton

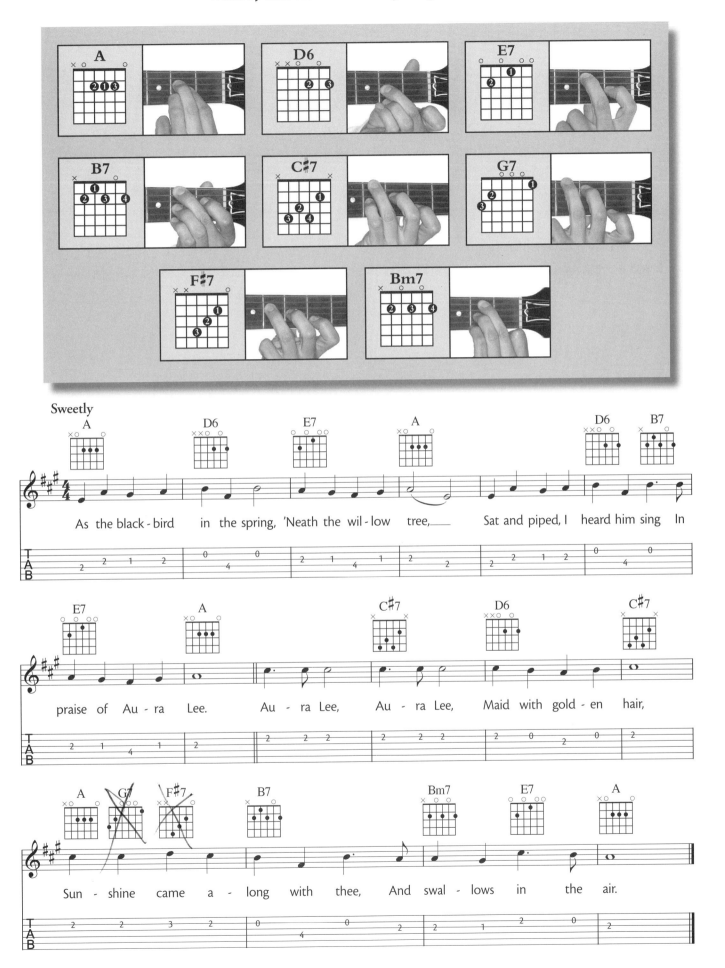

AULD LANG SYNE

Words by Robert Burns • Scottish air

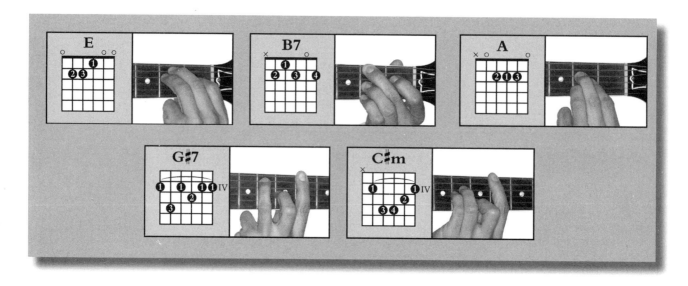

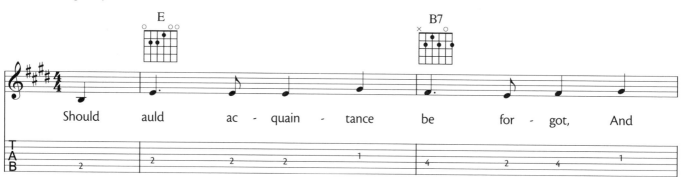

Nostalgically

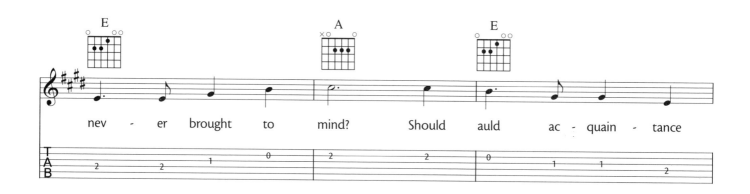

Should auld ac - quain - tance be for - got, And nev - er brought to mind? Should auld ac - quain - tance

2. We twa ha'e ran aboot the braes,
   And pu'd the gowans fine,
   We've wndered many a weary foot,
   Sin auld lang syne.
   Chorus

3. We twa ha'e sported i' the burn,
   Frae mornin' sun till dine,
   But seas between us braid ha'e roared,
   Sin auld lang syne.
   Chorus

4. And here's a hand my trusty frien',
   And gie's a hand o' thine,
   We'll take a cup o' kindness yet,
   For auld lang syne.
   Chorus

5. Should auld acquaintance be forgot,
   And never brought to mind?
   Should auld acquaintance be forgot,
   And days of auld lang syne?
   Chorus

BABY, WON'T YOU PLEASE COME HOME?

Words and music by Charles Warfield and Clarence Williams

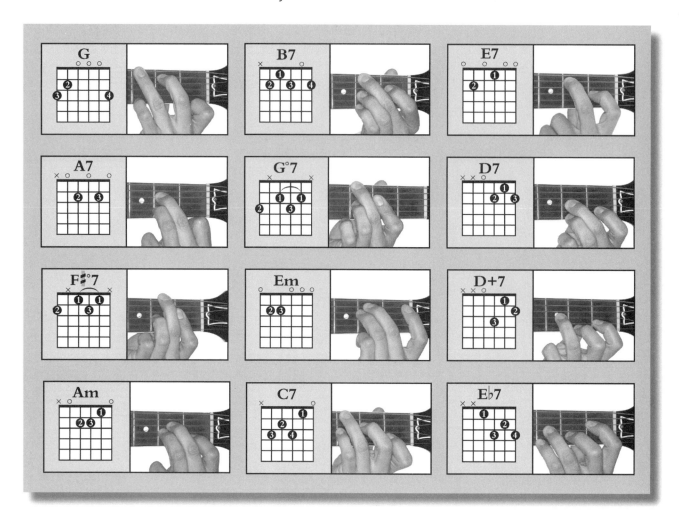

With a steady beat

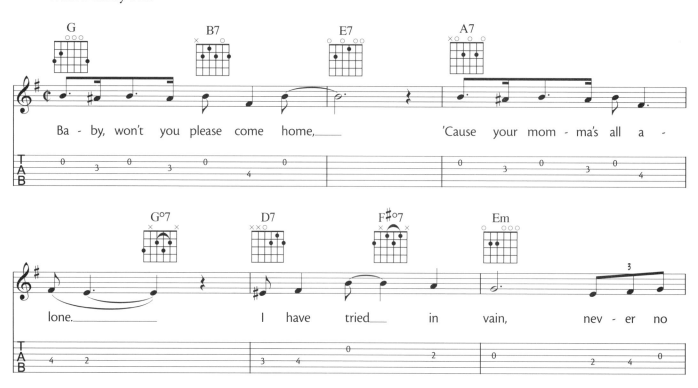

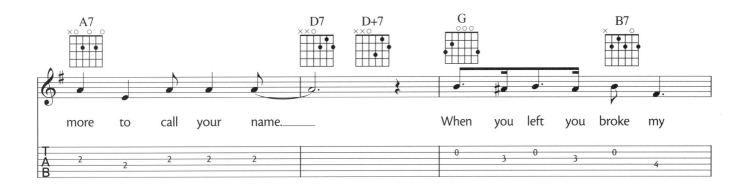

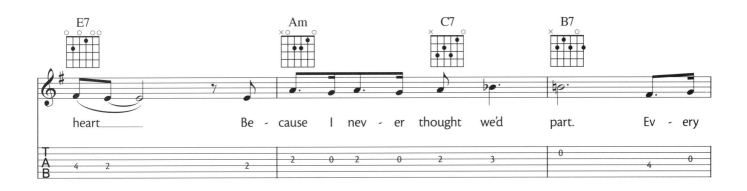

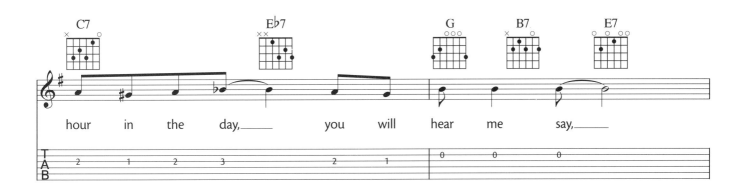

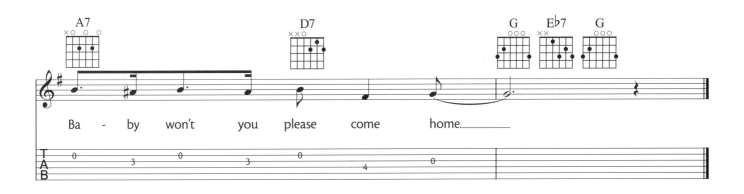

BACK HOME AGAIN IN INDIANA

Words by Ballard MacDonald • Music by James Hanley

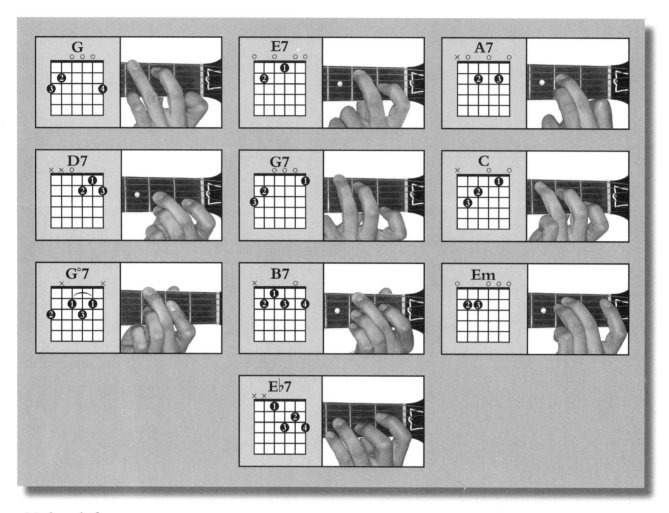

Moderately fast

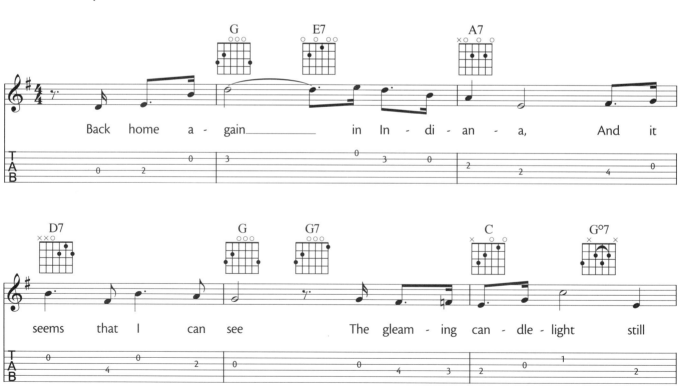

Back home a - gain_____ in In - di - an - a, And it

seems that I can see The gleam - ing can - dle - light still

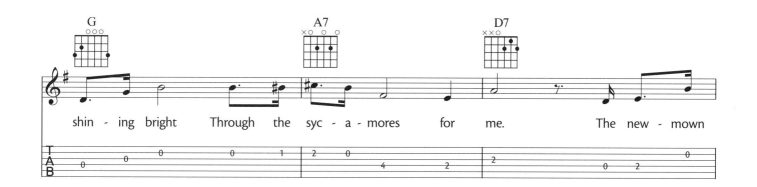

shin - ing bright Through the syc - a - mores for me. The new - mown

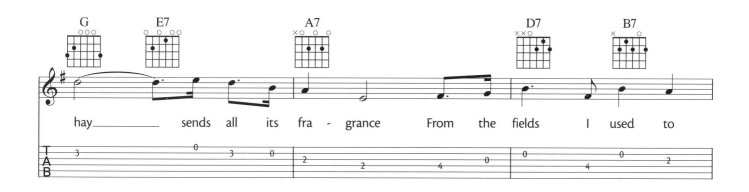

hay_____ sends all its fra - grance From the fields I used to

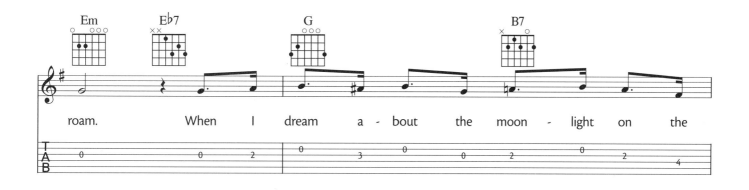

roam. When I dream a - bout the moon - light on the

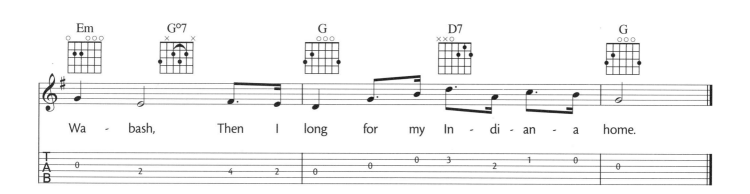

Wa - bash, Then I long for my In - di - an - a home.

BALLIN' THE JACK

Words by James Henry Burris • Music by Chris Smith

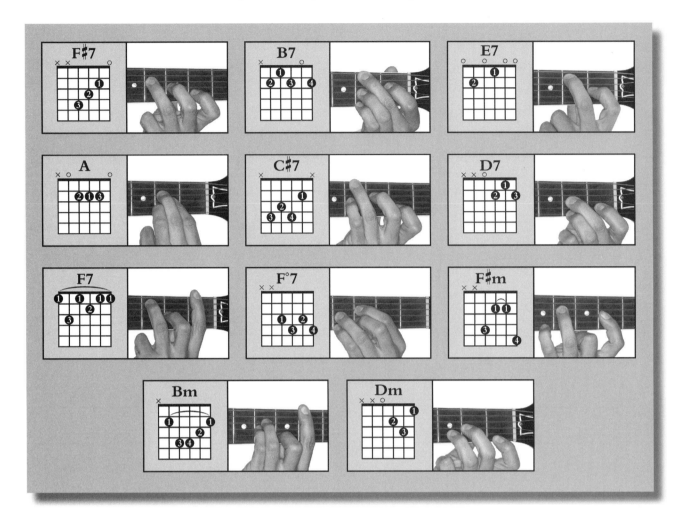

With a bounce

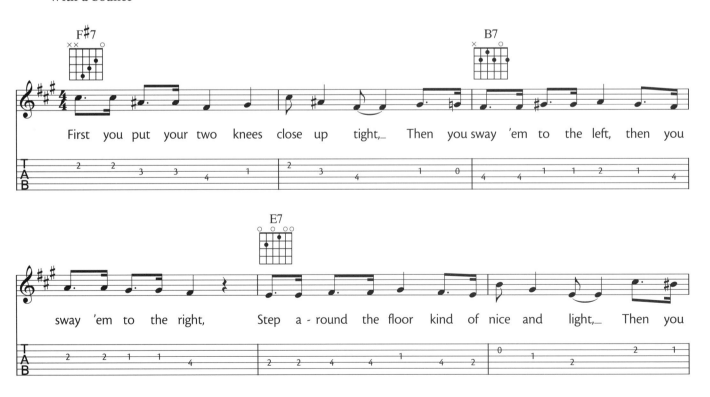

First you put your two knees close up tight,_ Then you sway 'em to the left, then you

sway 'em to the right, Step a-round the floor kind of nice and light,_ Then you

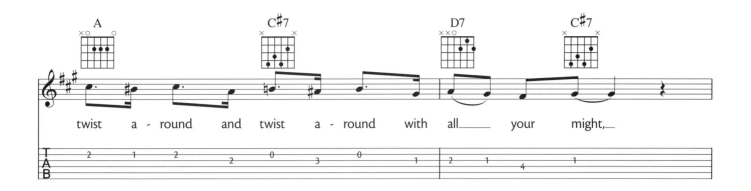

twist a - round and twist a - round with all___ your might,___

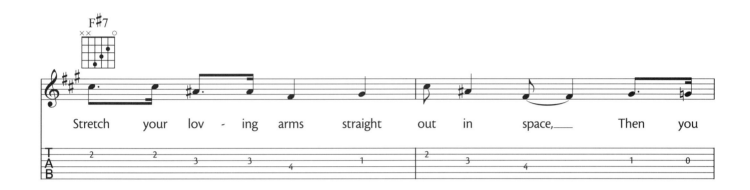

Stretch your lov - ing arms straight out in space,___ Then you

do the "Ea - gle Rock" with___ style and grace,___ Swing your foot way 'round then

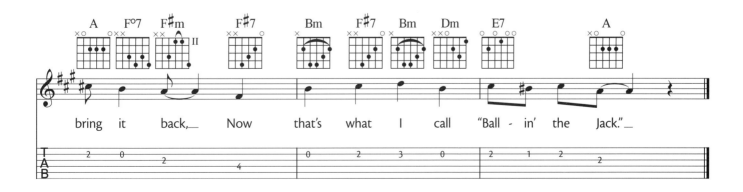

bring it back,___ Now that's what I call "Ball - in' the Jack."___

LA BAMBA

Mexican dance

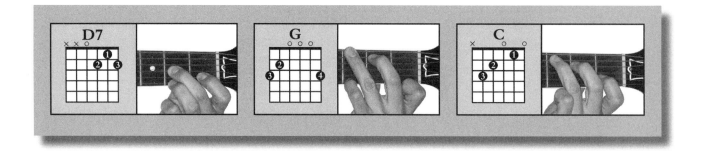

With a Latin beat

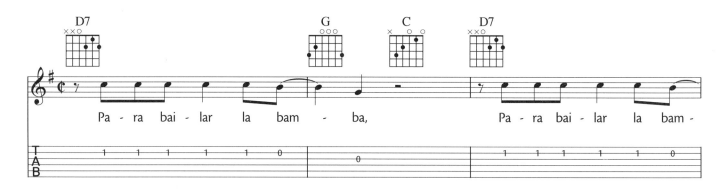

Pa - ra bai - lar la bam - ba, Pa - ra bai - lar la bam -

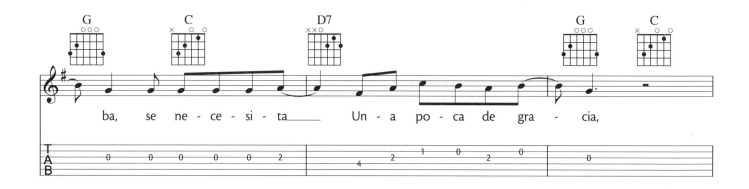

ba, se ne - ce - si - ta___ Un - a po - ca de gra - cia,

Un - a po - ca de gra - cia, par' mi par' tia. Ay ar - ri - ba, y ar - ri - ba.

THE BAND PLAYED ON

Words by John E. Palmer • Music by Charles B. Ward

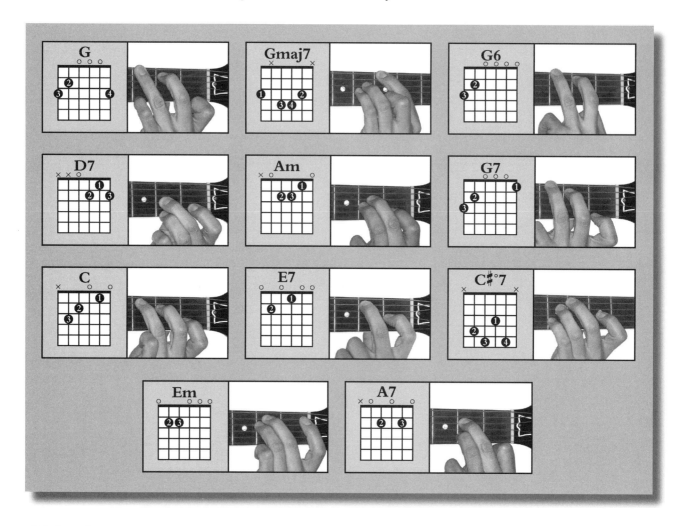

Moderately

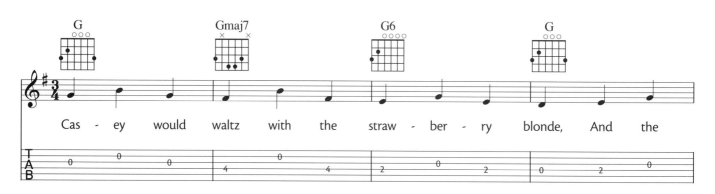

Cas - ey would waltz with the straw - ber - ry blonde, And the

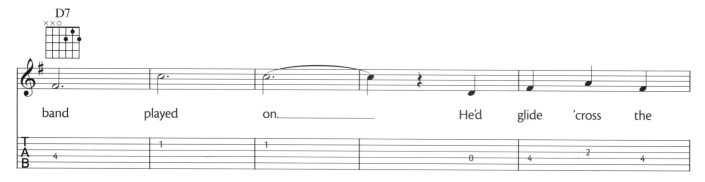

band played on._____ He'd glide 'cross the

BARBARA ALLEN

English ballad

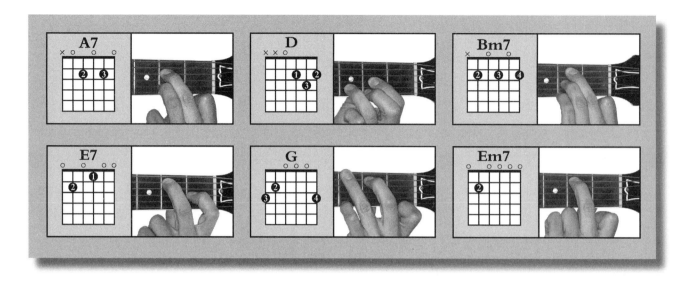

Slowly

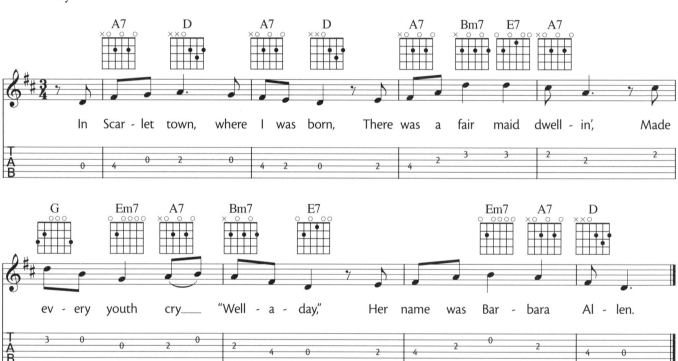

In Scar-let town, where I was born, There was a fair maid dwell-in', Made ev-ery youth cry___ "Well-a-day," Her name was Bar-bara Al-len.

2. 'Twas in the merry month of May,
   When green buds they were swellin';
   Sweet William on his deathbed lay,
   For love of Barbara Allen.

3. Well slowly, slowly got she up,
   And slowly went she nigh him;
   But all she said as she passed his bed,
   "Young man, I think you're dying."

4. She walked out in the green , green fields,
   She heard his death bells knellin',
   And every stroke it seemed to say,
   "Hard-hearted Barbara Allen.

5. "Oh father, father, dig my grave,
   Go dig it deep and narrow.
   Sweet William died for me today;
   I'll die for him tomorrow.

6. They buried her in the old churchyard,
   Sweet William's grave was nigh her,
   And from his heart grew a red, red rose,
   And from her heart, a briar.

7. They grew and grew up the old church wall,
   'Til they could grow no higher,
   Until they tied a true-lovers' knot;
   The red rose and the briar.

BEALE STREET BLUES

Words and music by W.C. Handy

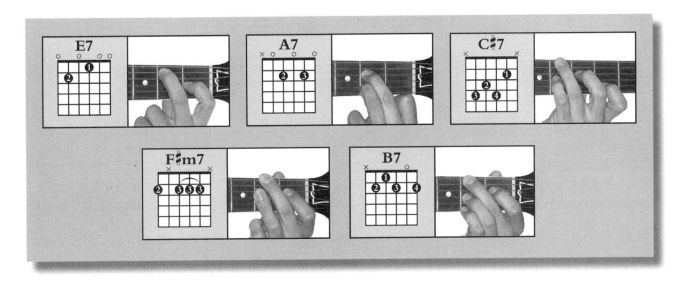

With a steady beat

BEAUTIFUL DREAMER

Words and music by Stephen C. Foster

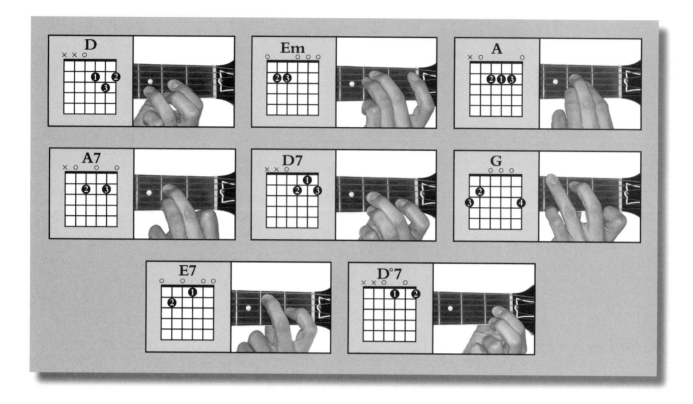

Gently

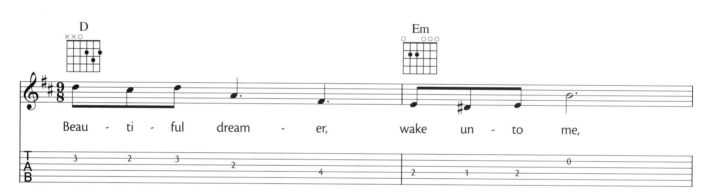

Beau - ti - ful dream - er, wake un - to me,

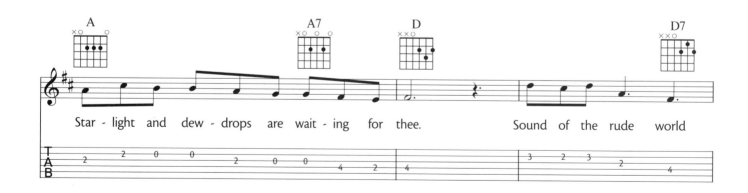

Star - light and dew - drops are wait - ing for thee. Sound of the rude world

THE BELLS OF ST. MARY'S

Words by Douglas Furber • Music by A. Emmett Adams

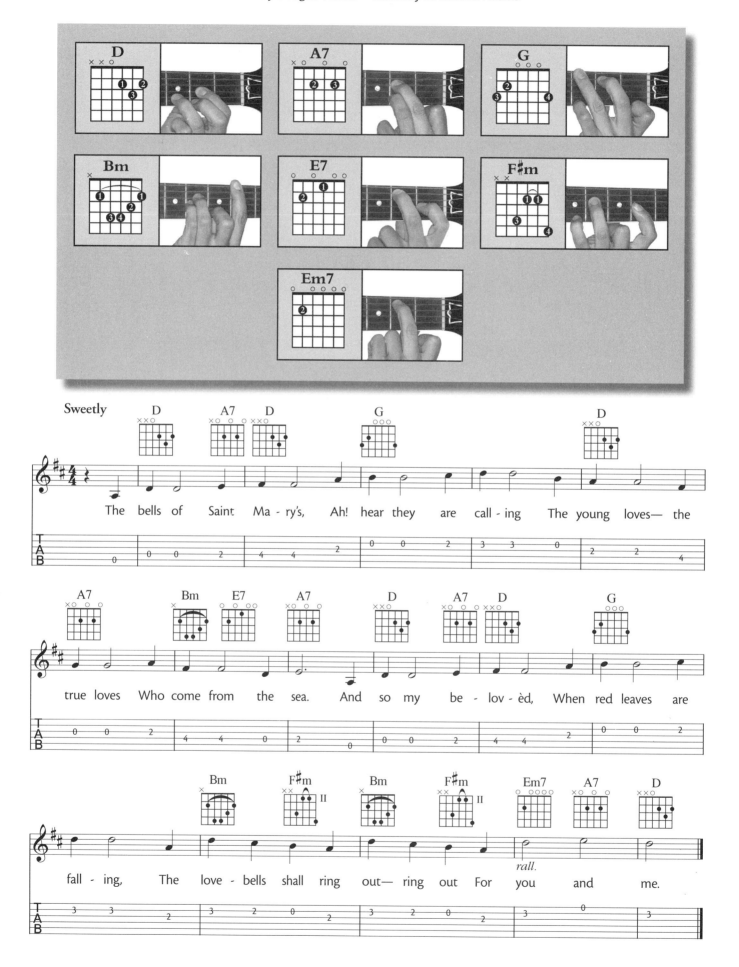

BRAHMS LULLABY

Words anonymous • Music by Johannes Brahms

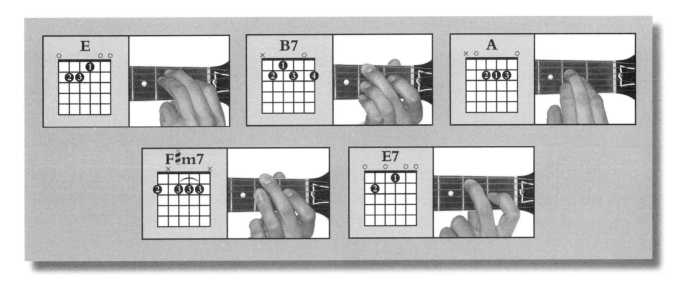

Slowly

Lull - a - by___ and good night, With ros - es___ de - light__ Creep in - to thy_ bed, There

pil - low thy head. If God will thou shalt wake, When the morn - ing doth

break,___ If God will, thou shalt wake, When the morn - ing doth break.

BILL BAILEY

Words and music by Hughie Cannon

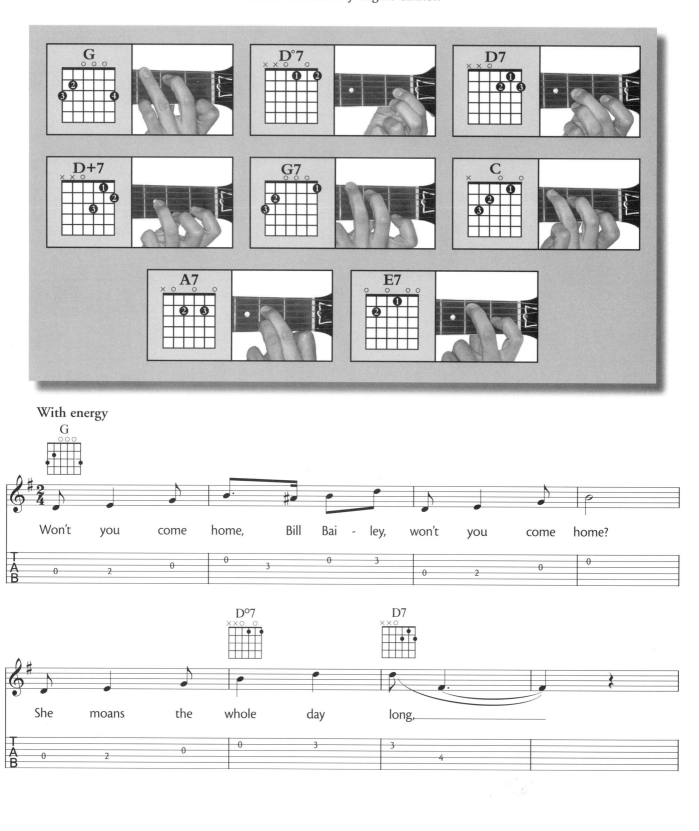

With energy

Won't you come home, Bill Bai - ley, won't you come home?

She moans the whole day long,

I'll do the cook - ing, dar - ling, I'll pay the rent,

BRIDAL CHORUS

Music by Richard Wagner

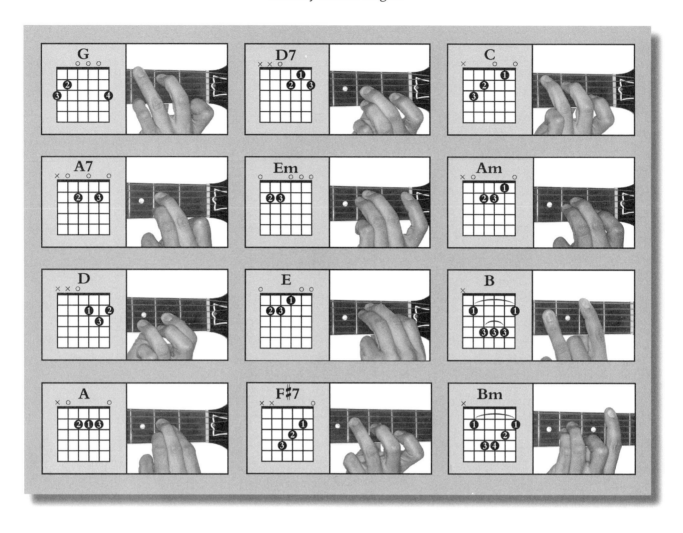

Solemnly

Guid - ed by us, thrice hap - py pair, En - ter the door - way, 'tis love that in - vites,

All that is brave, All that is fair, Love now tri - um - phant for - ev - er u - nites.

BURY ME NOT ON THE LONE PRAIRIE

American cowboy song

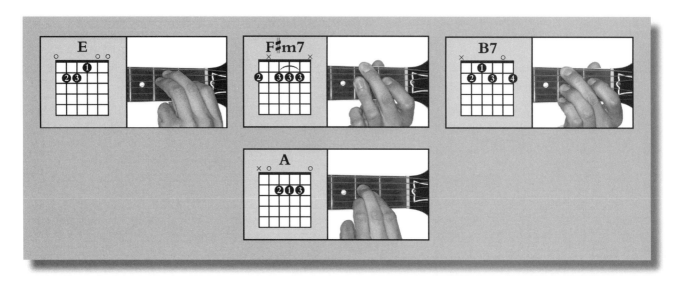

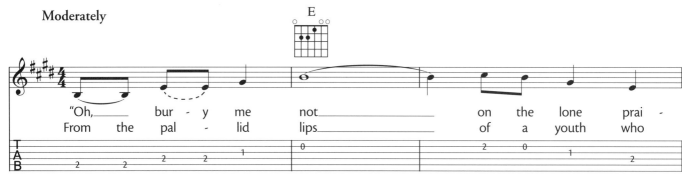

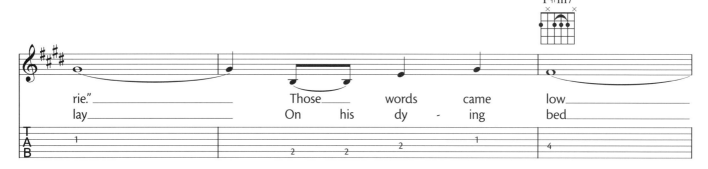

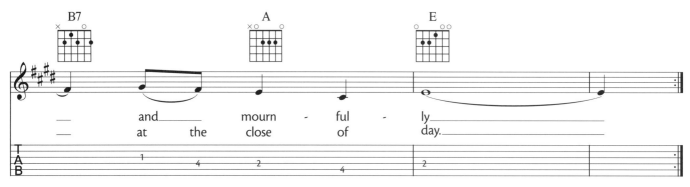

2. "Oh, bury me not"—and his voice failed there,
But we took no heed of his dying prayer.
In a narrow grave just six by three,
We buried him on the lone prairie.

3. And the cowboys now as they roam the plain,
(For they marked the spot where his bones were lain),
Fling a handful of roses o'er the grave,
With a prayer to Him who his soul will save.

BY THE LIGHT OF THE SILVERY MOON

Words by Edward Madden • Music by Gus Edwards

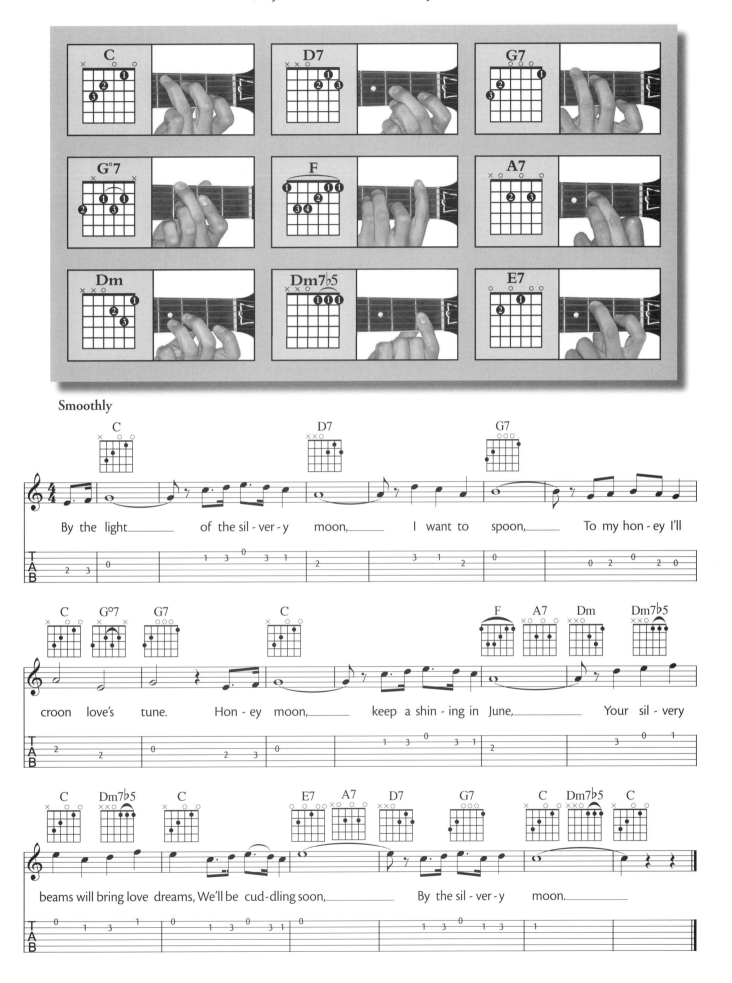

Smoothly

By the light_____ of the sil - ver - y moon,_____ I want to spoon,_____ To my hon - ey I'll

croon love's tune. Hon - ey moon,_____ keep a shin - ing in June,_____ Your sil - very

beams will bring love dreams, We'll be cud - dling soon,_____ By the sil - ver - y moon.

C.C. RIDER

American blues

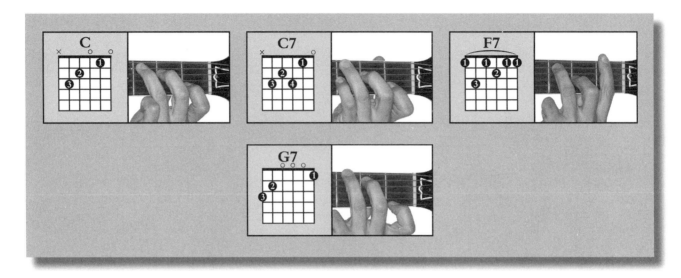

With a driving beat

2. C.C. Rider, love you, 'deed I do,
C.C. Rider, love you, 'deed I do,
There isn't one thing, darlin', I wouldn't do for you.

3. C.C. Rider, I need you by my side,
C.C. Rider, I need you by my side,
You're the only one who keeps me satisfied.

CARELESS LOVE

American blues

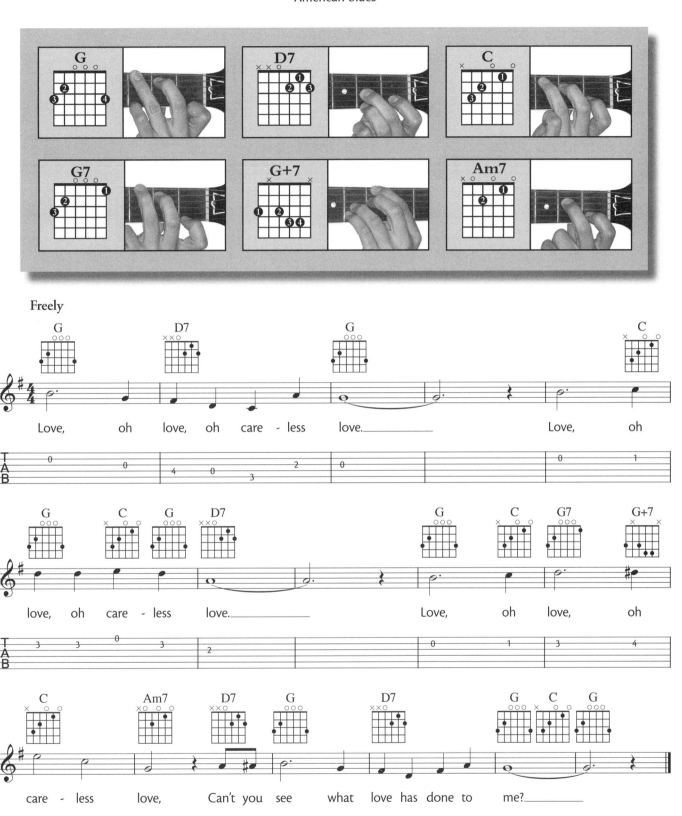

Freely

Love, oh love, oh care - less love._____ Love, oh

love, oh care - less love._____ Love, oh love, oh

care - less love, Can't you see what love has done to me?_____

2. I was happy as can be,
Days were sunny, bright, and free.
You came along to do me wrong,
And you brought your careless love to me.

3. I cried last night and the night before,
Cried last night and the night before,
Cried last night and the night before,
Gonna cry tonight, and cry no more.

CAROLINA IN THE MORNING

Words by Gus Kahn • Music by Walter Donaldson

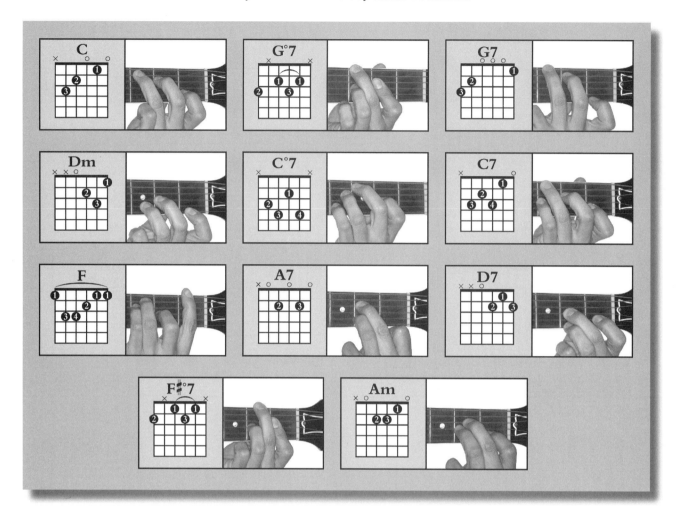

Moderately

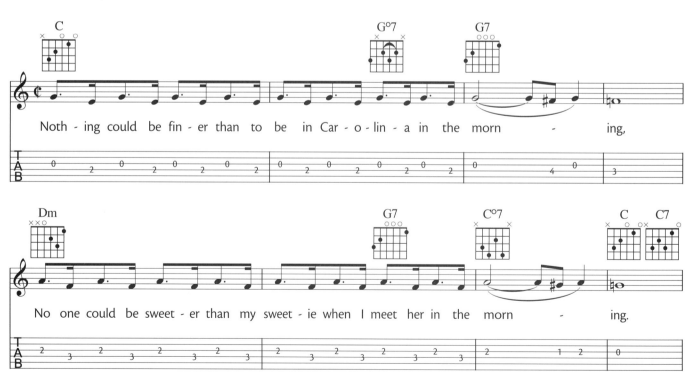

Noth - ing could be fin - er than to be in Car - o - lin - a in the morn - ing,

No one could be sweet - er than my sweet - ie when I meet her in the morn - ing.

CHICAGO (THAT TODDLIN' TOWN)

Words and music by Fred Fisher

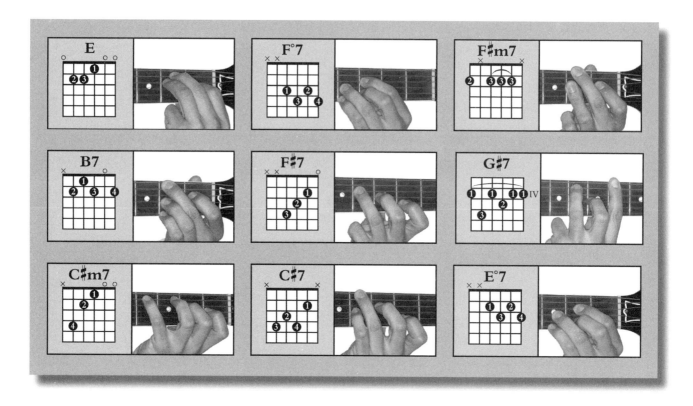

Moderately fast

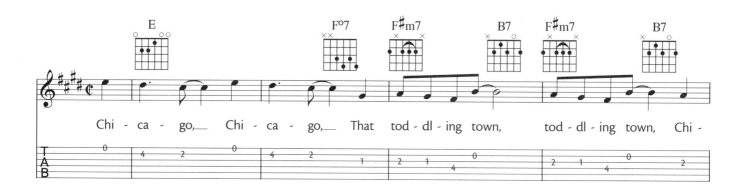

Chi - ca - go,___ Chi - ca - go,___ That tod - dl - ing town, tod - dl - ing town, Chi -

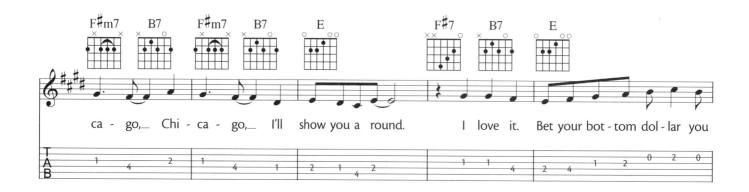

ca - go,___ Chi - ca - go,___ I'll show you a round. I love it. Bet your bot - tom dol - lar you

CHINATOWN, MY CHINATOWN

Words by William Jerome • Music by Jean Schwartz

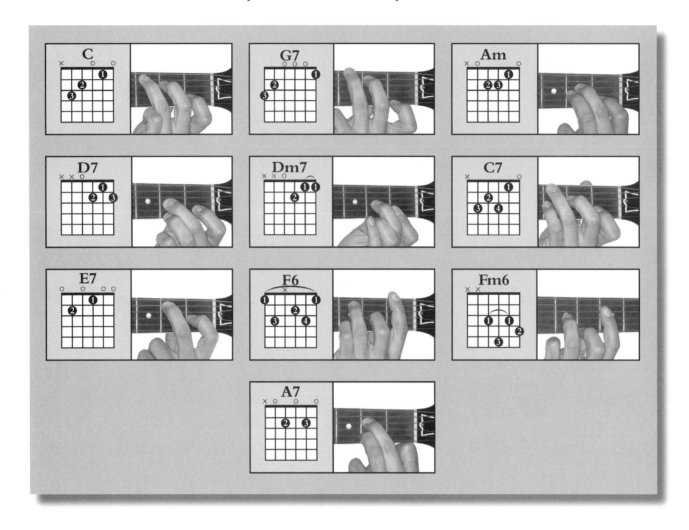

Moderately

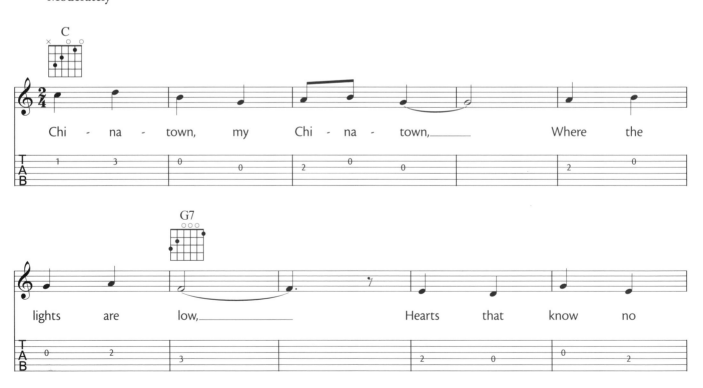

CIRIBIRIBIN

Words and music by Alberto Pestalozza

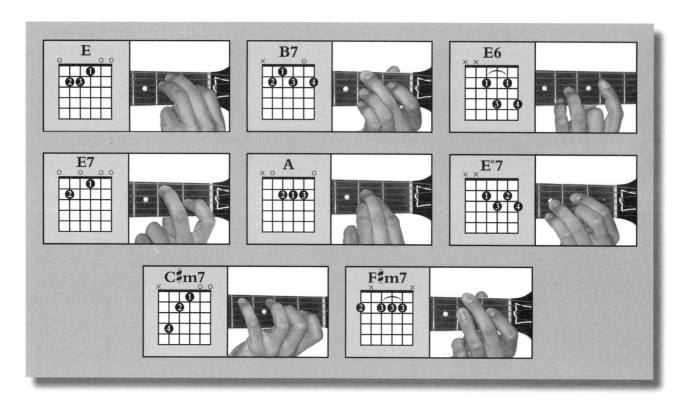

Lively

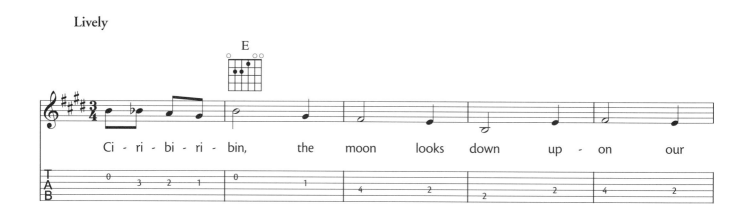

Ci - ri - bi - ri - bin, the moon looks down up - on our

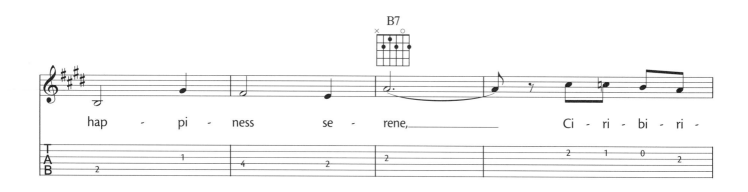

hap - pi - ness se - rene,_____ Ci - ri - bi - ri -

COLORADO TRAIL

American cowboy song

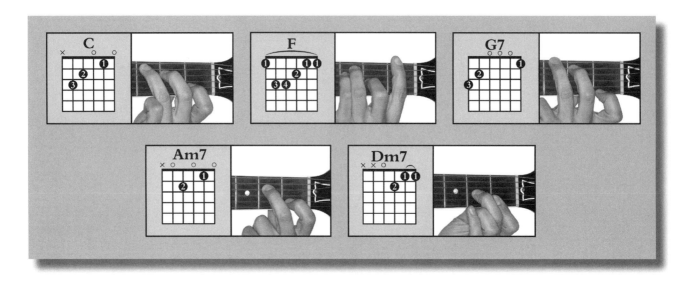

Moderately

Eyes like a morn-ing star, Cheeks like a rose, Lau-ra was a pret-ty girl,

God Al-might-y knows. Weep all you lit-tle rains, Wail, winds,

wail, All a-long, a-long, a-long That Col-o-ra-do Trail.

COMIN' THROUGH THE RYE

Words by Robert Burns • Scottish air

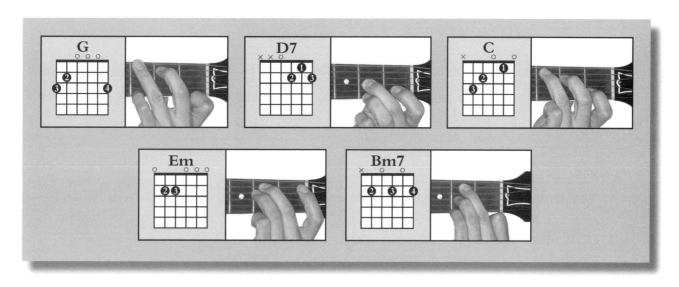

COME BACK TO SORRENTO

Words and music by Ernesto de Curtis & Claude Aveling

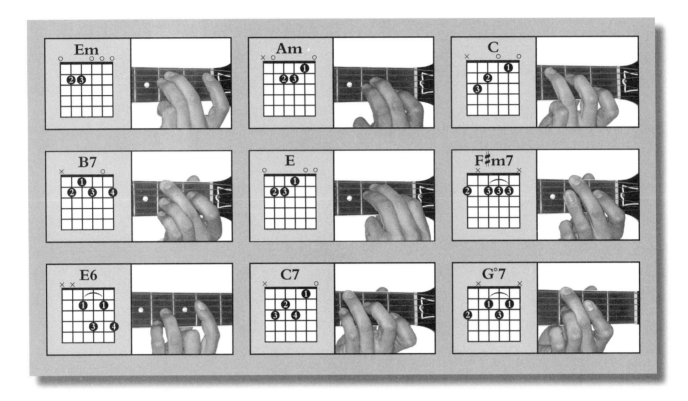

Freely

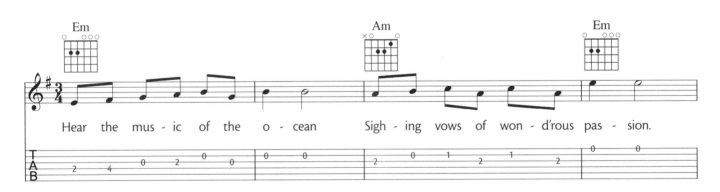

Hear the mus-ic of the o-cean Sigh-ing vows of won-d'rous pas-sion.

Vows dear, like of you I'm think-ing In my dreams tho' I'm a-wake.

CORINNA, CORINNA

American blues

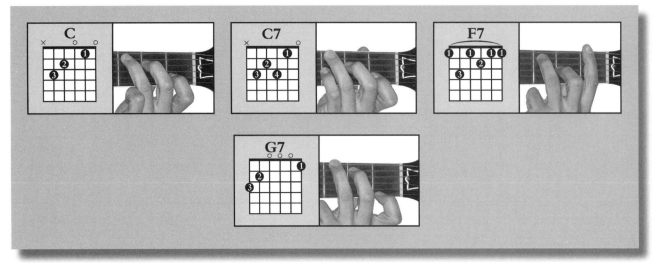

With a steady beat

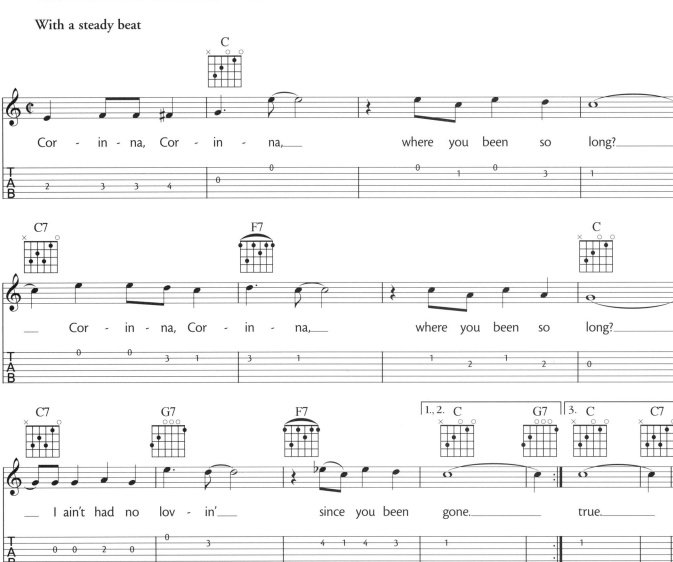

Cor - in - na, Cor - in - na,___ where you been so long?___

___ Cor - in - na, Cor - in - na,___ where you been so long?___

___ I ain't had no lov - in'___ since you been gone.___ true.___

2. Corinna, Corinna, where'd you go last night?
   Corinna, Corinna, where'd you go last night?.
   Your shoes ain't buttoned, girl; don't fit you right.

3. Corinna, Corinna, love you, 'deed I do.
   Corinna, Corinna, love you, 'deed I do.
   But, honey, what's the use? You can't be true.

THE CRUEL WAR

American ballad

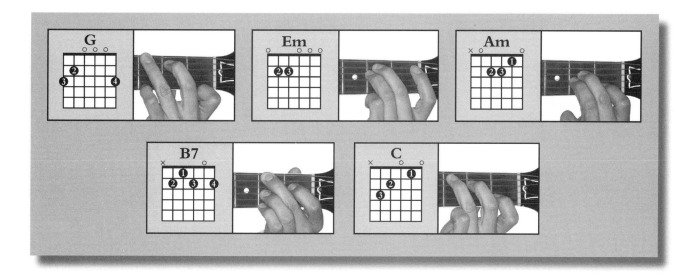

Slowly

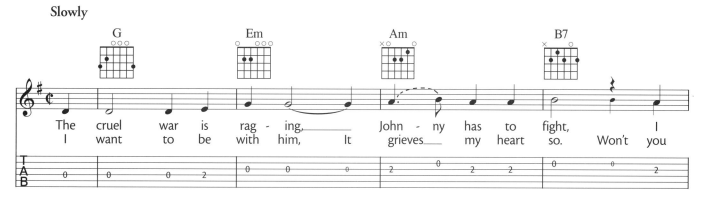

The cruel war is rag - ing,_____ John - ny has to fight, I
I want to be with him, It grieves_____ my heart so. Won't you

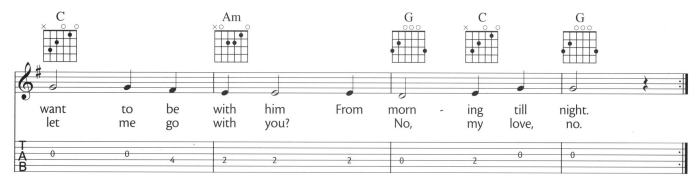

want to be with him From morn - ing till night.
let me go with you? No, my love, no.

2. I'd go to your captain, get down on my knees,
And a thousand gold guineas I'd pay for your release.
A thousand gold guineas, it grieves my heart so.
Won't you let me go with you? No, my love, no.

3. Tomorrow is Sunday, Monday is the day,
That your captain will call you, and you must obey,
Your captain will call you, it grieves my heart so.
Won't you let me go with you? No, my love, no.

4. I'll tie back my hair, men's clothing I'll put on,
And I'll pass as your comrade as we march along.
I'll pass as your comrade, no one will ever know.
Won't you let me go with you? No, my love, no.

5. Oh Johnny, oh Johnny, I fear you are unkind,
For I love you far better than all of mankind.
I love you far better than words can e'er express,
Won't you let me go with you? Yes, my love, yes.

DANNY BOY

Irish folk song

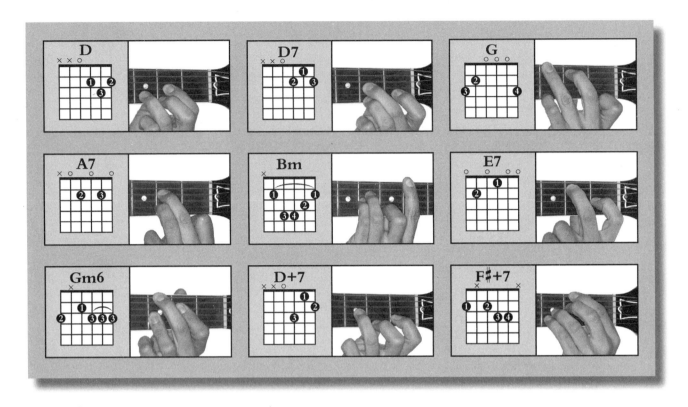

With feeling

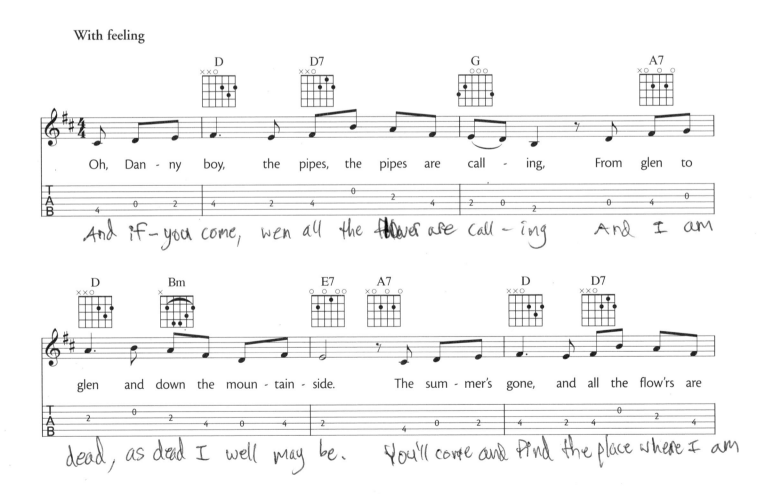

Oh, Dan-ny boy, the pipes, the pipes are call-ing, From glen to

And if-you come, wen all the flower are call-ing And I am

glen and down the moun-tain-side. The sum-mer's gone, and all the flow'rs are

dead, as dead I well may be. You'll come and find the place where I am

dy - ing, 'Tis you, 'tis you, must go and I must bide. But come ye

ly – ing And need to say an "Ave" the for me. And I shall

back when sum - mer's in the mead - ow, Or when the val - ley's hushed and white with

here, though soft you tread above me And all my dreams will warm and

snow. 'Tis I'll be there in sun - light or in

sweeter be. If you only tell that you love me

shad - ow, Oh, Dan - ny boy, oh, Dan - ny boy, I love you so.

rall.

— me Then I will sleep in peace until you come to me.

2. And if you come when all the flowers are dying,
And I am dead, as dead I well may be,
You'll come and find the place where I am lying,
And kneel and say an 'Ave' there for me.
And I shall hear, though soft you tread above me,
And all my dreams will warm and sweeter be.
If you only tell me that you love me,
Then I will sleep in peace until you come to me.

DARK EYES

Russian Gypsy folk song

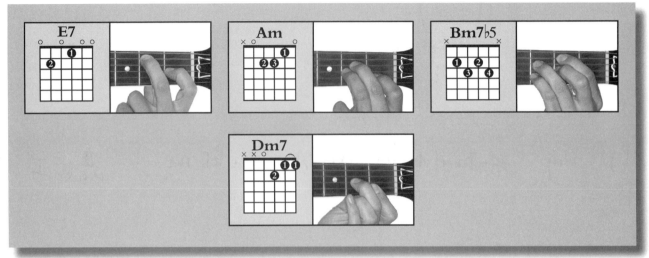

Freely

Eyes of ec - sta - sy,___ Al - ways haunt - ing me,___ Al - ways haunt - ing me___ With your

mys - ter - y.___ Tell me ten - der - ly,___ You be - long to me___

___ For e - ter - ni - ty,___ Dark eyes, talk to me.___

DOWN IN THE VALLEY

American folk song

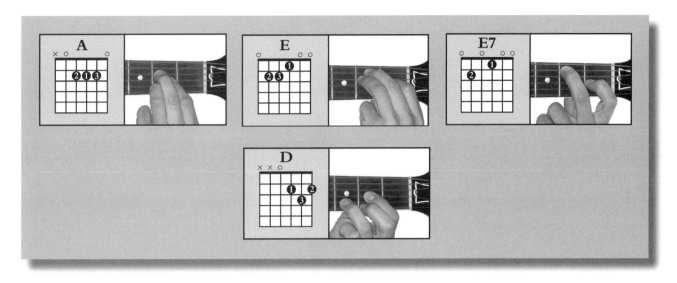

Freely

Down in the val - ley, the val - ley so

low, Hang your head o -

ver, Hear the wind blow.

2. Roses love sunshine, violets love dew,
   Angels in heaven know I love you.
   Know I love you, dear, know I love you.
   Angels in heaven know I love you.

3. Build me a castle forty feet high,
   So I may see him as he rides by,
   As he rides by, love, as he rides by,
   So I may see him as he rides by.

DEEP RIVER

American spiritual

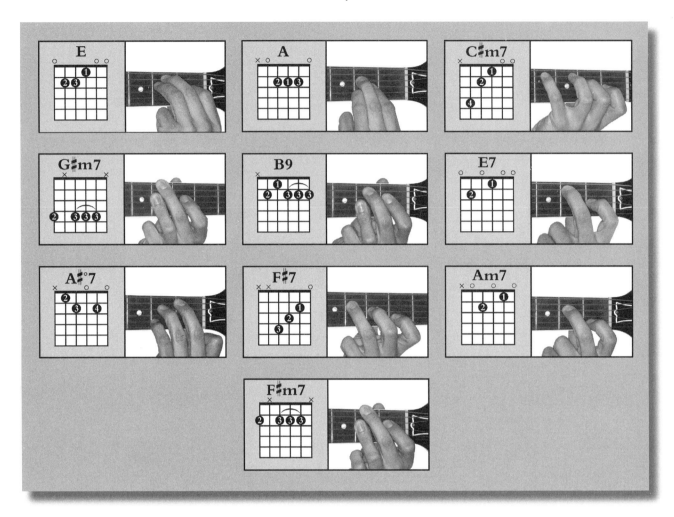

Slowly

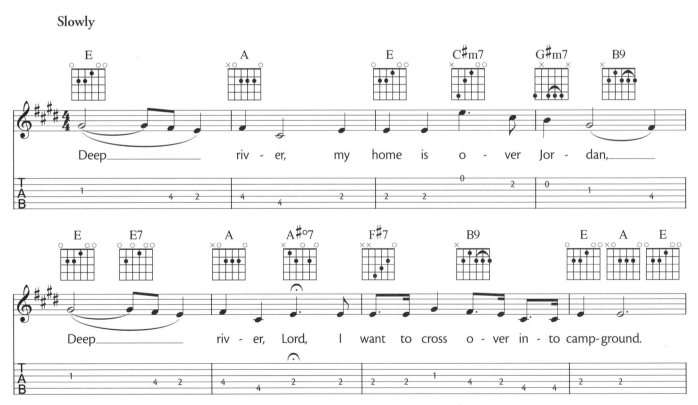

Deep_____ riv - er, my home is o - ver Jor - dan,_____

Deep_____ riv - er, Lord, I want to cross o - ver in - to camp-ground.

DOWN BY THE OLD MILL STREAM

Words and music by Earl K. Smith & Tell Taylor

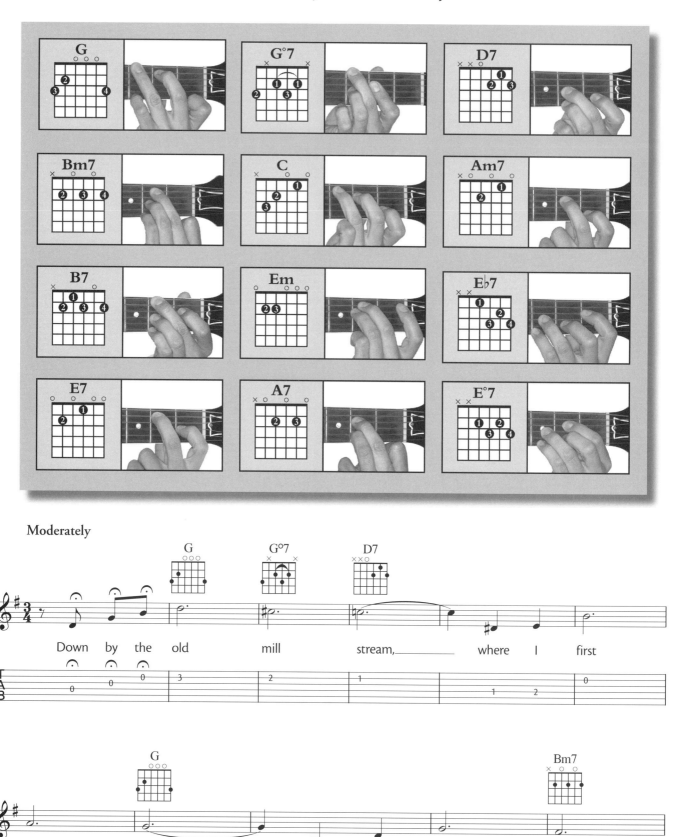

Moderately

Down by the old mill stream,_____ where I first

met you,_____ With your eyes of

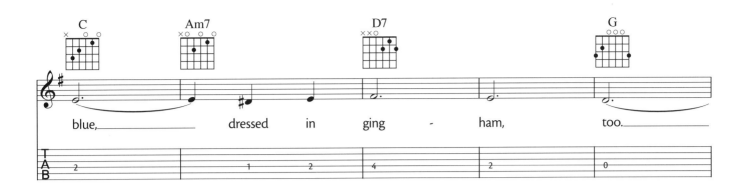

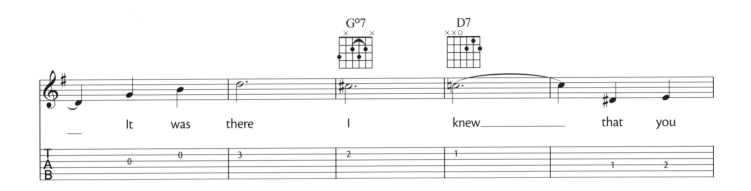

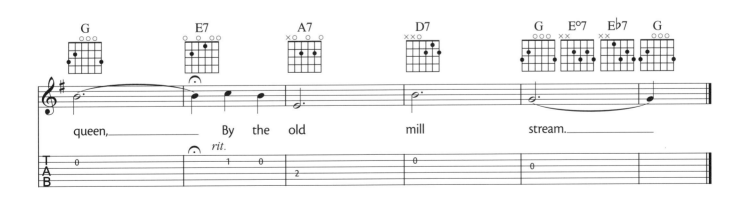

DOWN BY THE RIVERSIDE

American spiritual

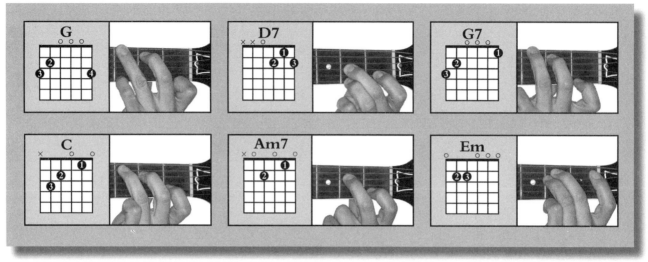

With a steady beat

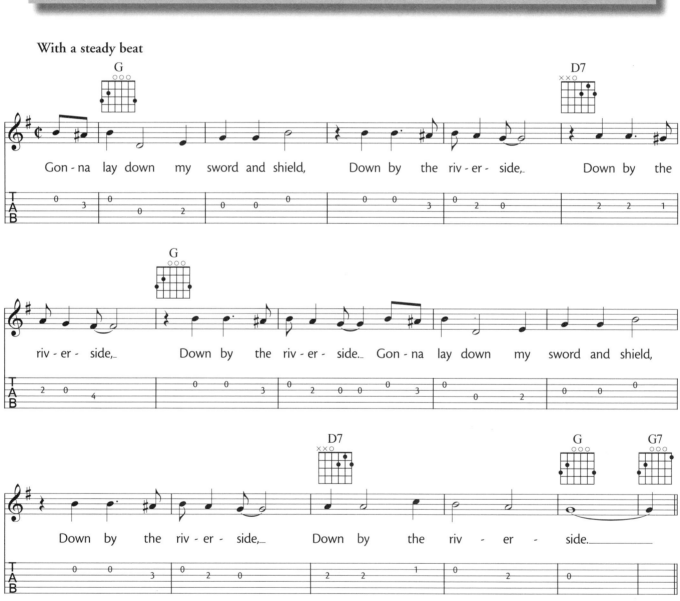

Gon - na lay down my sword and shield, Down by the riv - er - side,_ Down by the

riv - er - side,_ Down by the riv - er - side._ Gon - na lay down my sword and shield,

Down by the riv - er - side,_ Down by the riv - er - side._____

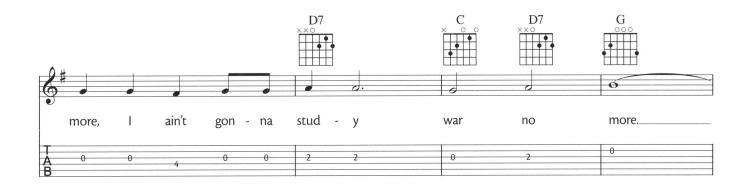

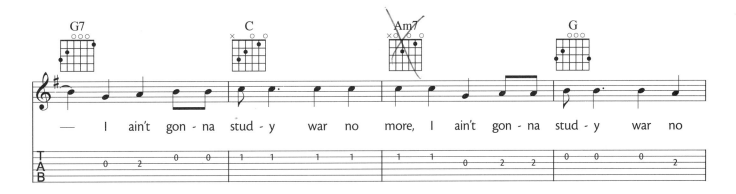

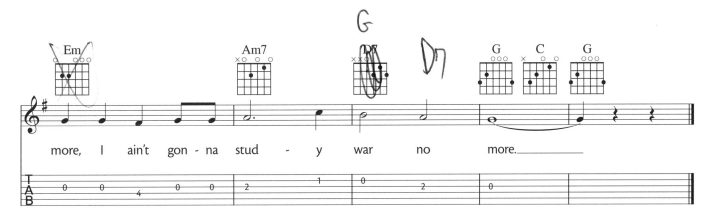

2. I'm gonna shake hands around the world,
Down by the riverside, (three times)
I'm gonna shake hands around the world,
And study war no more.
Chorus

DRINK TO ME ONLY WITH THINE EYES

Words by Ben Johnson • English air

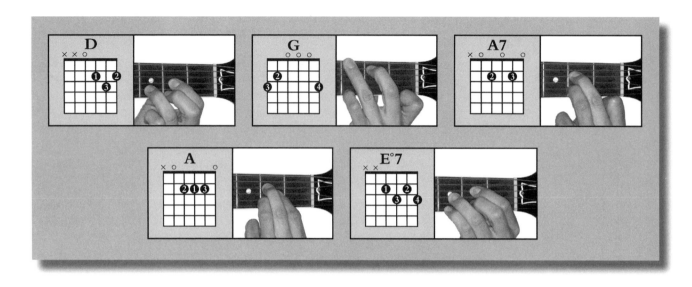

Slowly

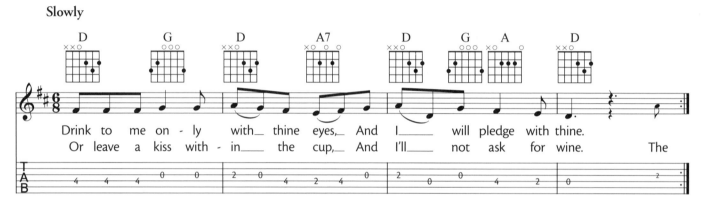

Drink to me on - ly with__ thine eyes,__ And I__ will pledge with thine.
Or leave a kiss with - in__ the cup,__ And I'll__ not ask for wine. The

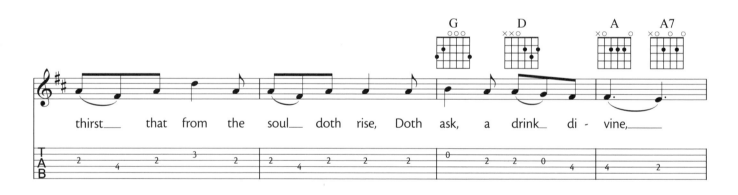

thirst__ that from the soul__ doth rise, Doth ask, a drink di - vine,_____

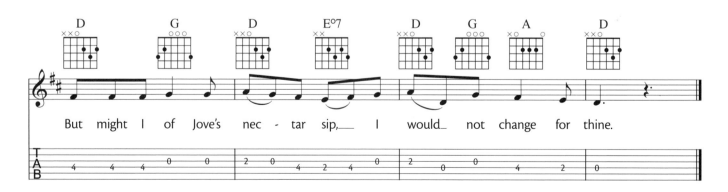

But might I of Jove's nec - tar sip,__ I would__ not change for thine.

EARLY ONE MORNING

English folk song

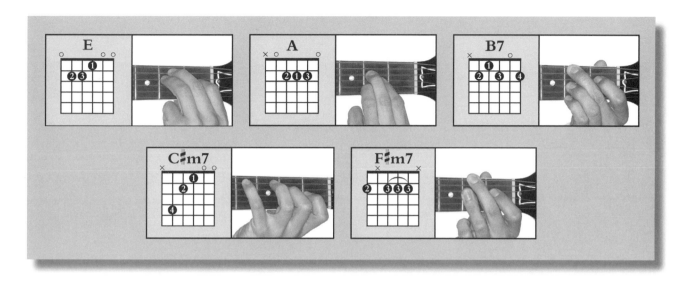

Sweetly

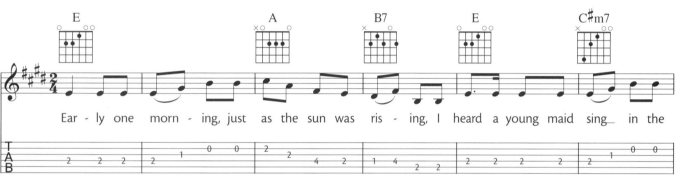

Ear - ly one morn - ing, just as the sun was ris - ing, I heard a young maid sing__ in the

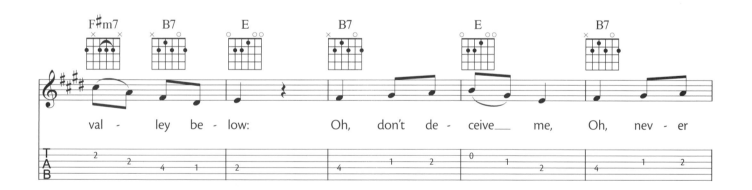

val - ley be - low: Oh, don't de - ceive__ me, Oh, nev - er

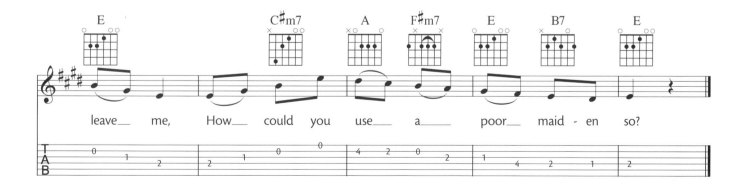

leave__ me, How__ could you use__ a__ poor__ maid - en so?

THE EDDYSTONE LIGHT

American folk song

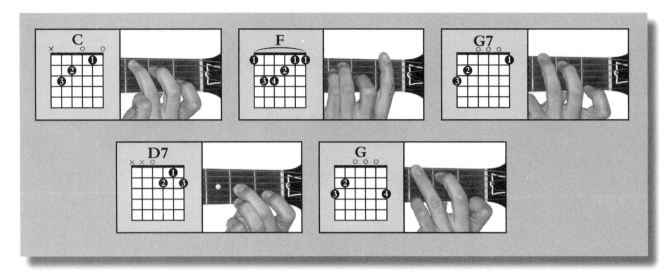

Briskly

My fa-ther was the keep-er of the Ed-dy-stone Light, He court-ed a mer-maid one fine night. From this un-i-on, there came three: A por-poise and a por-gy and the oth-er was me.

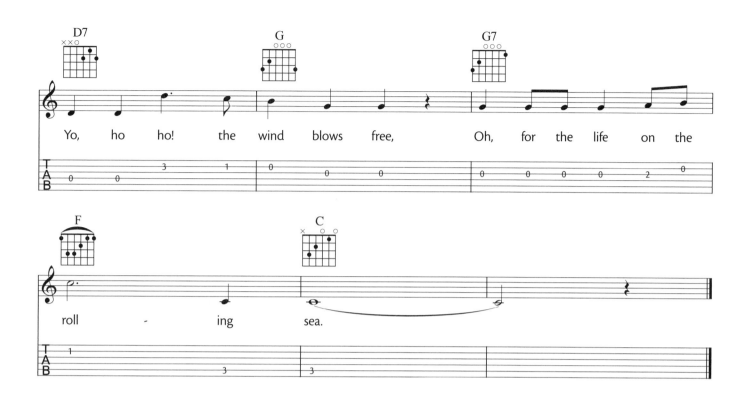

Yo, ho ho! the wind blows free, Oh, for the life on the

roll - ing sea.

2. One night while I was trimmin' of the glim,
   Singing a verse of the evening hymn,
   A voice from the starboard shouted "Ahoy!"
   There was my mother sittin' on a buoy.
   Chorus

3. "Oh, what has become of my children three?"
   My mother then she asked of me.
   "One was exhibited as a talking fish,
   And the other was served on a chafing dish."
   Chorus

4. Then the phosphorus flashed in her seaweed hair,
   I looked again, my mother wasn't there.
   A voice came echoing out of the night,
   "To the devil with the keeper of the Eddystone Light!"
   Chorus

THE ERIE CANAL

American folk song

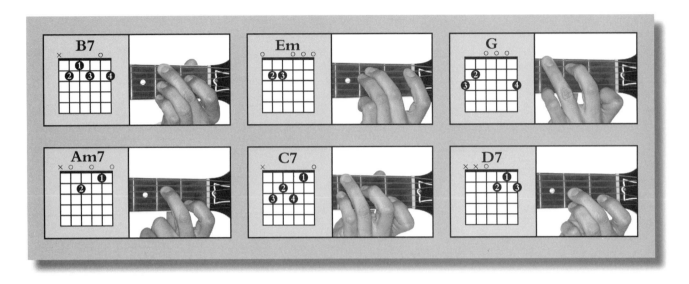

With a steady beat

FOR ME AND MY GAL

Words by Edgar Leslie and E. Ray Goetz • Music by George W. Meyer

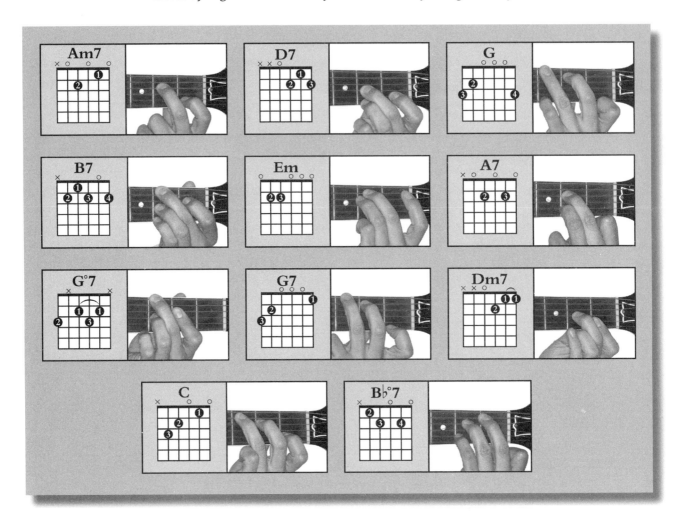

Moderately

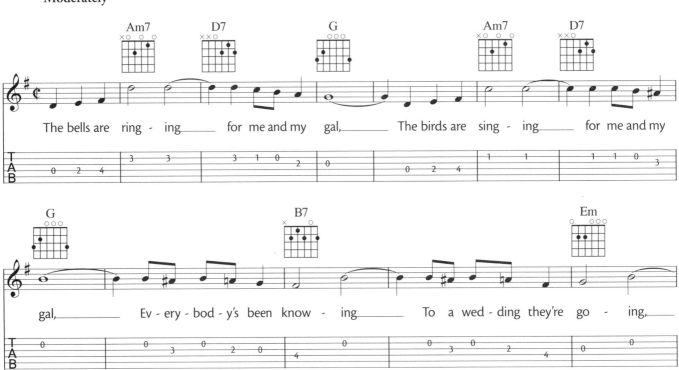

The bells are ring - ing_____ for me and my gal,_____ The birds are sing - ing_____ for me and my

gal,_____ Ev - ery - bod - y's been know - ing_____ To a wed - ding they're go - ing,_____

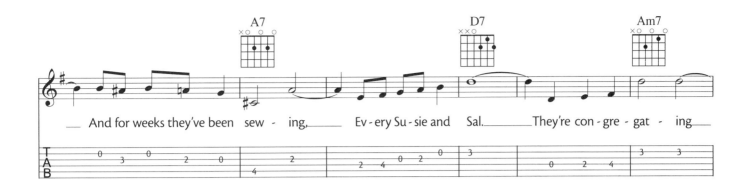

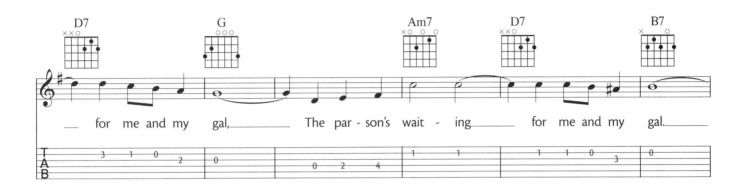

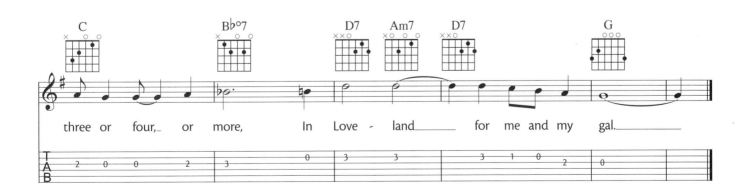

FOR HE'S A JOLLY GOOD FELLOW

Words anonymous • French air

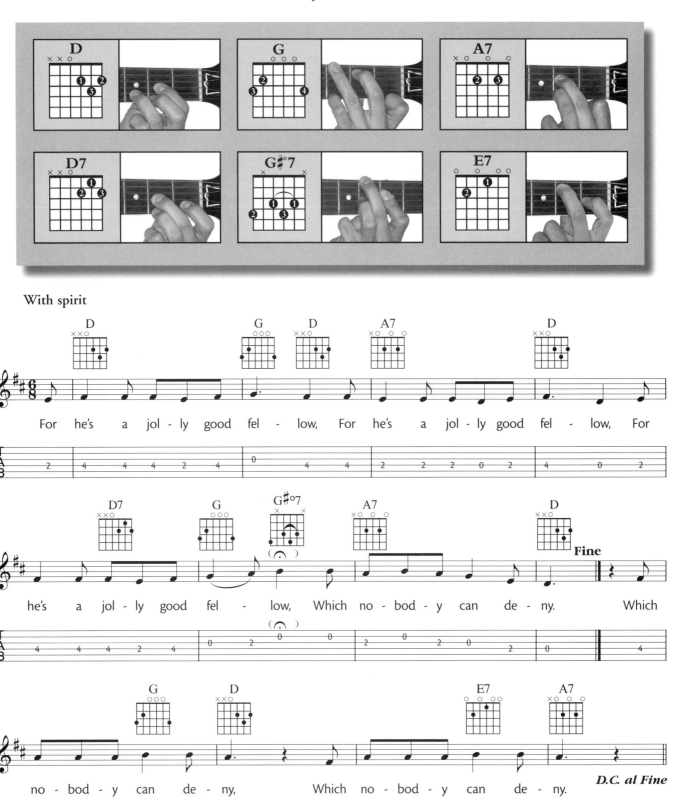

With spirit

For he's a jol-ly good fel-low, For he's a jol-ly good fel-low, For

he's a jol-ly good fel-low, Which no-bod-y can de-ny. Which

no-bod-y can de-ny, Which no-bod-y can de-ny.

D.C. al Fine

FROGGY WENT A-COURTIN'

American folk song

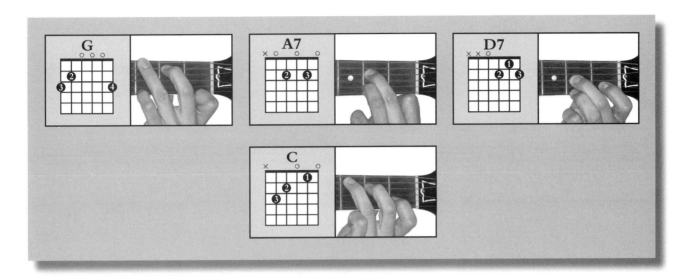

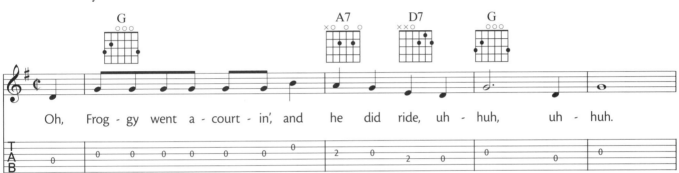

Moderately

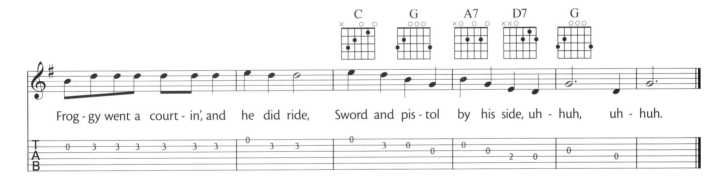

Oh, Frog-gy went a-court-in', and he did ride, uh-huh, uh-huh.

Frog-gy went a court-in', and he did ride, Sword and pis-tol by his side, uh-huh, uh-huh.

2.. Well, he rode down to Miss Mouse's door, uh-huh, u-huh,
Well, he rode down to Miss Mouse's door,
Where he had often been before, uh-huh, uh-huh.

3. He took Miss Mousie on his knee, *etc.*
Said, "Miss Mousie will you marry me?" *etc.*

4. "I'll have to ask my Uncle Rat,"
"See what he will say to that."

5. "Without my Uncle Rat's consent,
"I would not marry the President."

6. Well, Uncle Rat rode off to town,
To buy his niece a wedding gown.

7. "Where will the wedding supper be?"
"Way down yonder in a hollow tree."

8. "What will the wedding supper be?"
"A fried mosquito and a roasted flea."

9. First to come in were two little ants
Fixing around to have a dance.

10. Next to come was a bumblebee,
Bouncing a fiddle on his knee.

11. And next to come was a big tomcat,
He chased the frog and the mouse and the rat.

THE FOX

American folk song

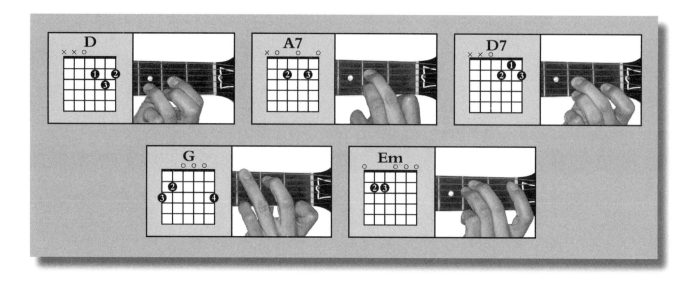

Quickly

The fox went out___ on a chill - y night,

Prayed for the moon for to give him light, For he'd

man - y a mile to go that night be -

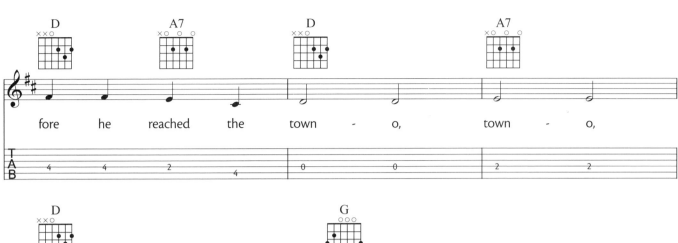

fore he reached the town - o, town - o,

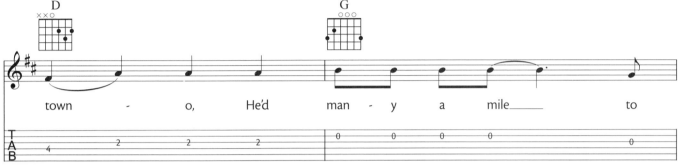

town - o, He'd man - y a mile_____ to

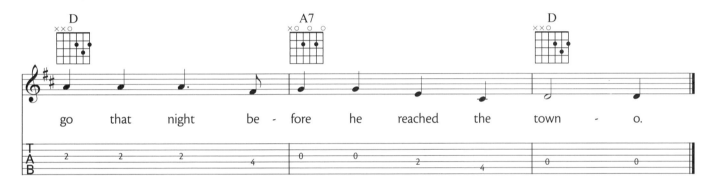

go that night be - fore he reached the town - o.

2. He ran till he came to a great big bin,
   The ducks and the geese were lying within,
   Said, "A couple of you will grease my chin,
   Before I leave this town-o," *etc.*

3. He grabbed the grey goose by the neck,
   Slung the little one over his back,
   He didn't mind their quack, quack, quack,
   And the legs all dangling down-o, *etc.*

4. Old mother pitter-patter jumped out of bed,
   Out of the window she cocked her head,
   Crying, "John, John, the grey goose is gone,
   And the fox is on the town-o," *etc.*

5. John, he went to the top of the hill,
   Blew his horn both loud and shrill;
   The fox, he said, "I'll flee with my kill
   He'll soon be on my trail-o, *etc.*

6. He ran till he came to his cozy den,
   There were the little ones, eight, nine, ten,
   They said daddy, you better go back again,
   'Cause it must be a mighty fine town-o, *etc.*

7. Then the fox and his wife, without any strife
   Cut up the goose with a carving knife,
   They've never had such a supper in their life,
   And the little ones chewed on the bones-o, *etc.*

FRANKIE AND JOHNNY

Words and music by Hughie Cannon

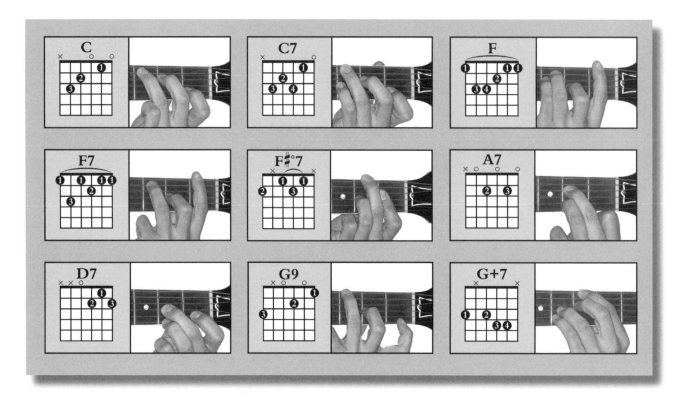

With a steady beat

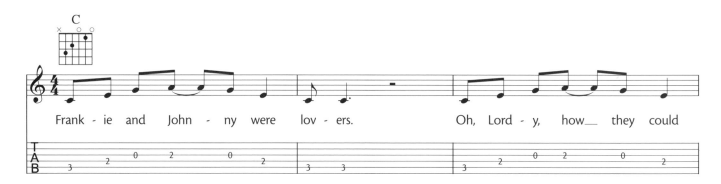

Frank - ie and John - ny were lov - ers. Oh, Lord - y, how___ they could

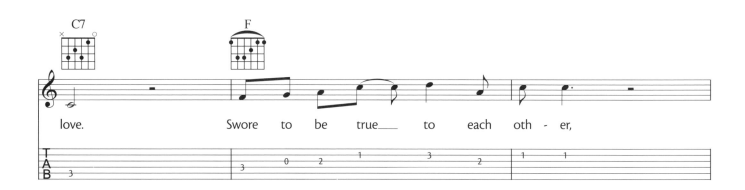

love. Swore to be true___ to each oth - er,

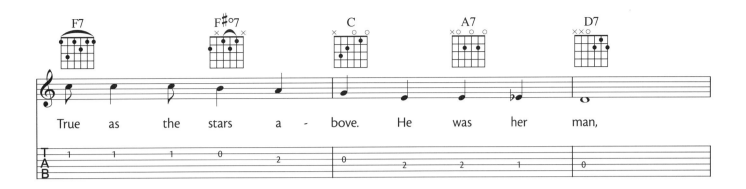

True as the stars a - bove. He was her man,

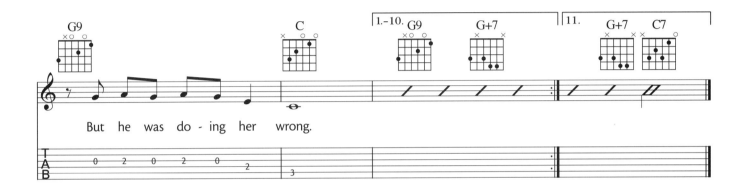

But he was do - ing her wrong.

2. Frankie and Johnny went walking.
   Johnny in his brand new suit.
   Oh, "Good Lord," says Frankie,
   "Don't my Johnny look cute."
   He was her man, but he done her wrong.

3. Frankie went down to the corner,
   Stopped in to buy her some beer
   Says to the big bartender,
   "Has my Johnny man been here?"
   He was her man, but he done her wrong.

4. "Well I ain't going to tell you no story,
   Aint' going to tell you no lie:
   Johnny went by 'bout an hour ago,
   With a girl named Nellie Bligh.
   He was her man, but he done her wrong.

5. Frankie went home to the hotel.
   She didn't go there for fun.
   Underneath her kimono
   She carried a forty-five gun.
   He was her man, but he's doin' you wrong.

6. Frankie looked over the transom
   To see what she could spy,
   There sat Johnny on the sofa
   Just loving up Nellie Bligh.
   He was her man, but he was doin' her wrong.

7. Frankie got down from the high stool
   She didn't want to see no more;
   Rooty-toot-toot, three times she shot
   Right through that hardwood door.
   He was her man, but he done her wrong.

8. Roll me over easy,
   Roll me over slow,
   Roll me over easy, boys.
   Why did she shoot so low?
   I was her man, but I done her wrong.

9. Bring out your long, black coffin,
   Bring out your funeral clothes,
   Johnny's gone and cashed his bad checks
   To the graveyard Johnny goes,
   He was her man, but he done her wrong.

10. Drive out your rubber-tired carriage,
    Drive out your rubber-tired hack,
    There's twelve men a-going to the graveyard
    And eleven coming back,
    He was her man, but he done her wrong.

11. Sheriff arrested poor Frankie,
    Took her to jail that same day.
    He locked her up in a dungeon cell
    And threw the key away,
    He was her man, but he done her wrong.

GIVE MY REGARDS TO BROADWAY

Words and music by George M. Cohan

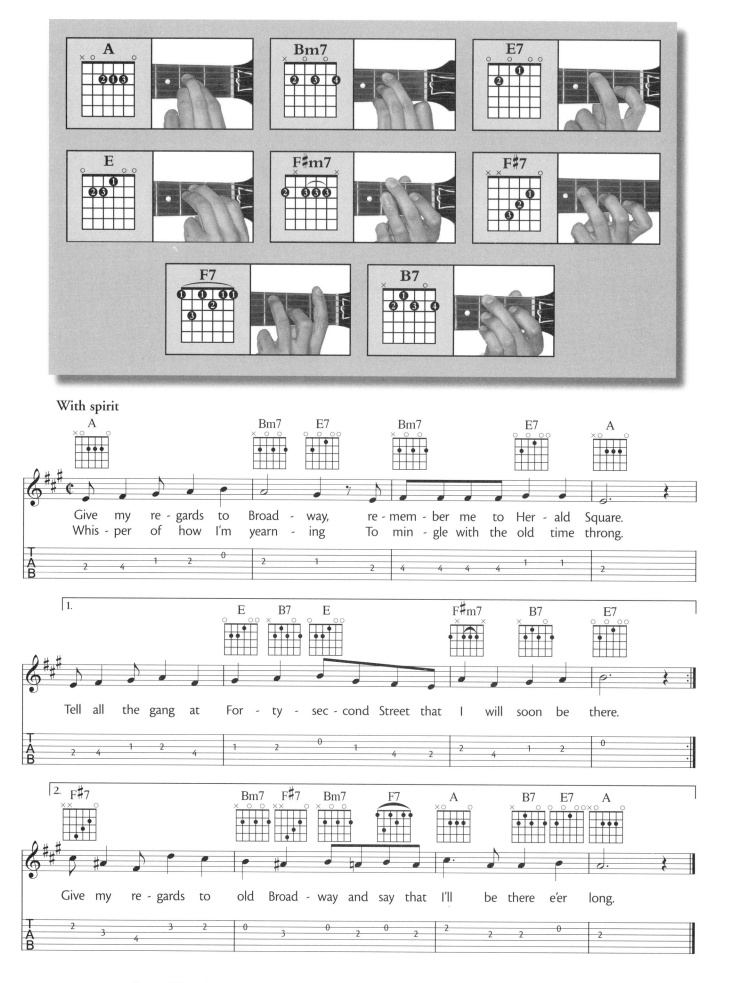

With spirit

Give my re - gards to Broad - way, re - mem - ber me to Her - ald Square.
Whis - per of how I'm yearn - ing To min - gle with the old time throng.

1.
Tell all the gang at For - ty - sec - cond Street that I will soon be there.

2.
Give my re - gards to old Broad - way and say that I'll be there e'er long.

GLOW WORM

Words and music by Paul Lincke

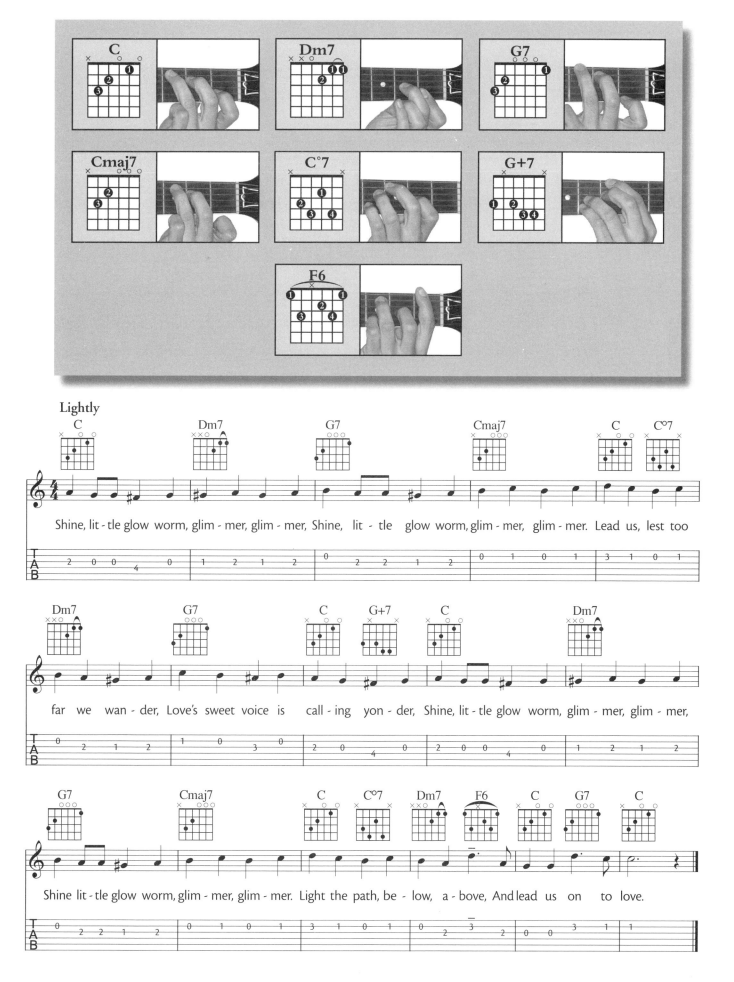

A GOOD MAN IS HARD TO FIND

Words and music by Eddie Green

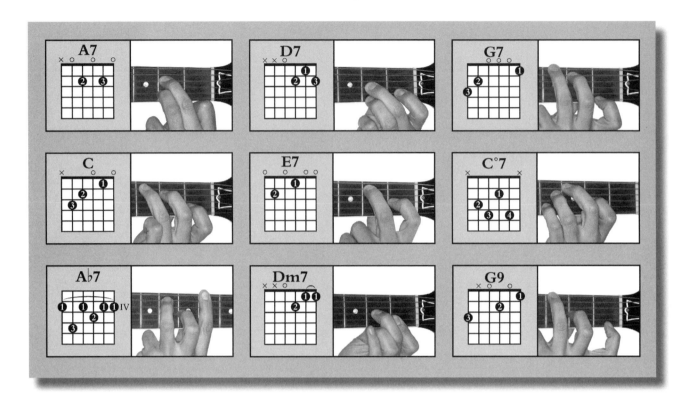

Moderately

A good man is hard to find, You al - ways get the oth - er

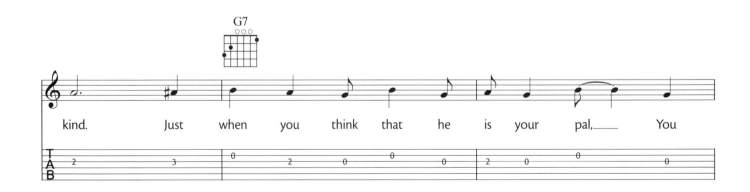

kind. Just when you think that he is your pal, You

GOOD MORNING BLUES

American blues

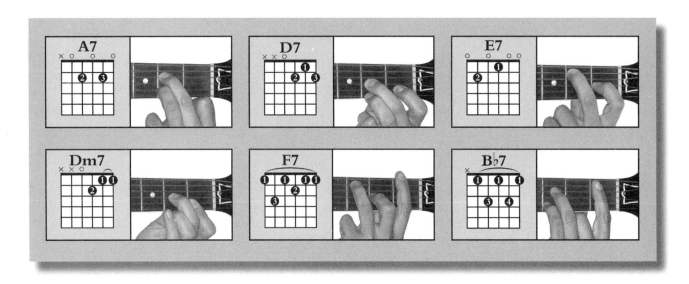

With a driving beat

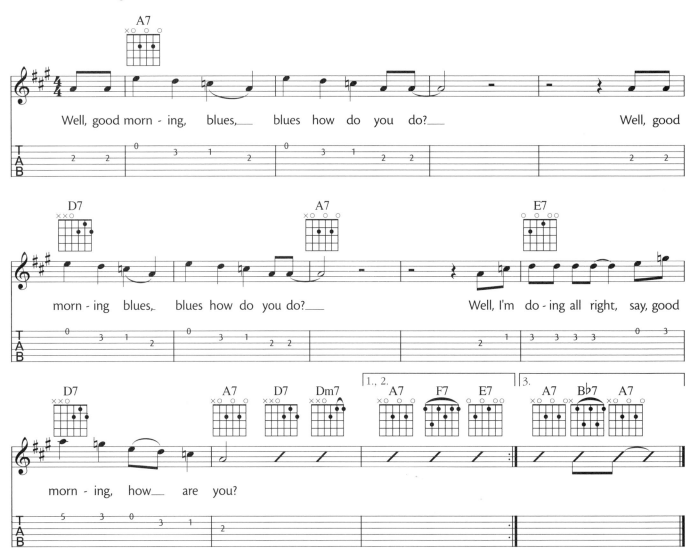

Well, good morn - ing, blues, blues how do you do? Well, good morn - ing blues, blues how do you do? Well, I'm do - ing all right, say, good morn - ing, how are you?

2.. I got up this morning, blues walkin' 'round my bed.
I got up this morning, blues walkin' 'round my bed.
Went to eat my breakfast, blues was in my bread.

3. I sent for you yesterday, here you come today.
I sent for you yesterday, here you come today.
You got your mouth wide open, you don't know
what to say.

GYPSY LOVE SONG

Words by Harry B. Smith • Music by Victor Herbert

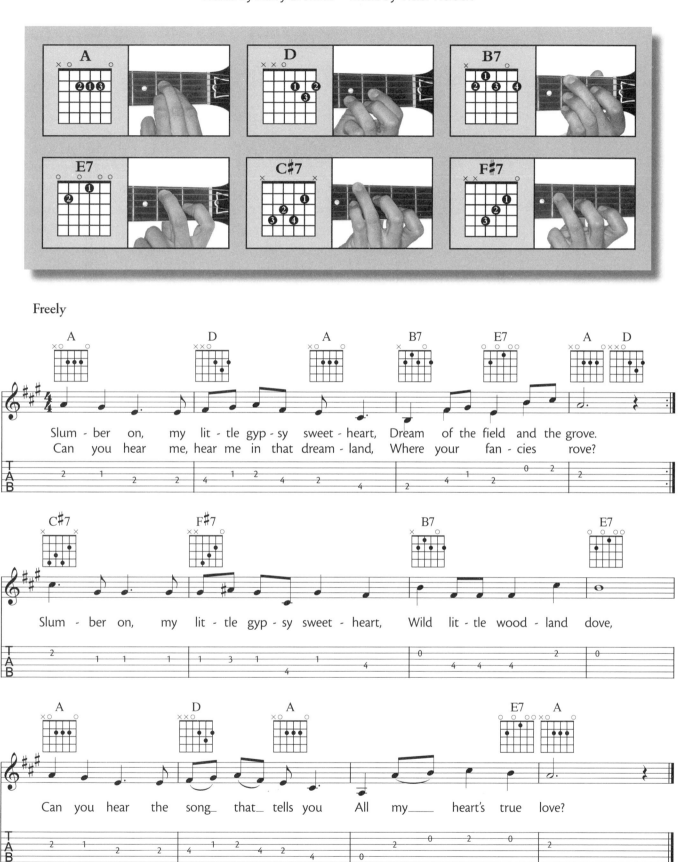

GREENSLEEVES

English folk song

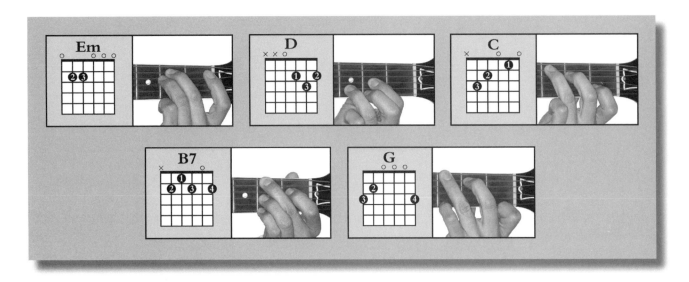

Gently

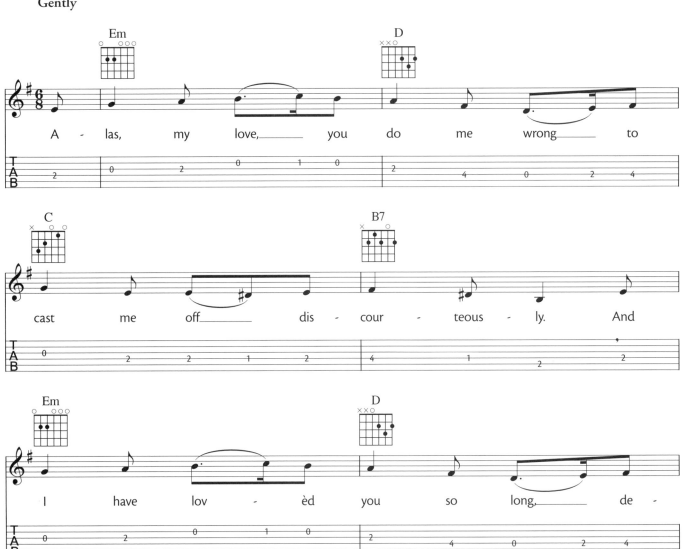

HAVAH NAGILAH

Israeli hora

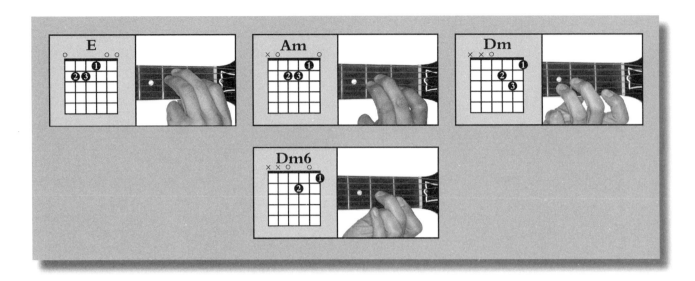

With a driving beat

Ha - vah_____ na - gi - lah, ha - vah_____ na - gil - ah, Ha - vah_____

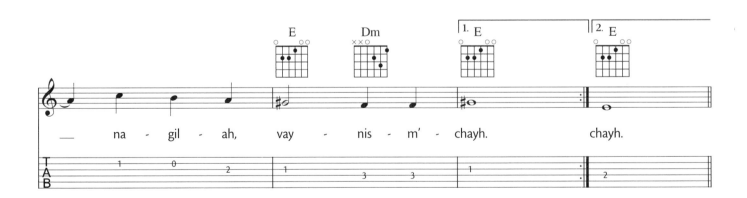

____ na - gil - ah, vay - nis - m' - chayh. chayh.

HAIL! HAIL! THE GANG'S ALL HERE

Words anonymous • Music by Arthur Sullivan

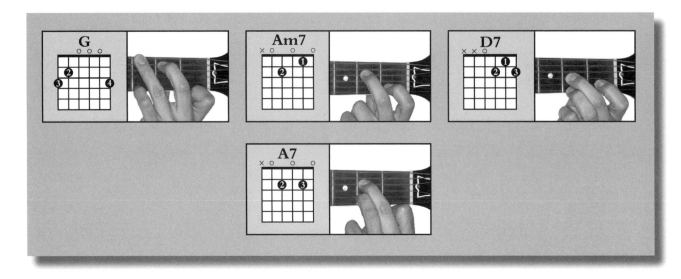

With a steady beat

Hail! Hail!____ the gang's all here. What the heck do we care,

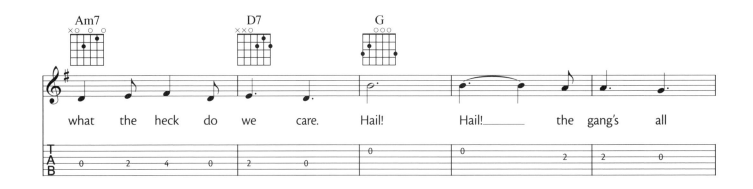

what the heck do we care. Hail! Hail!____ the gang's all

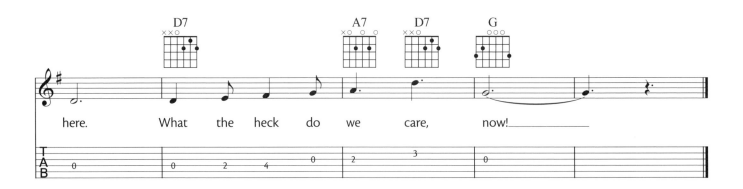

here. What the heck do we care, now!____

HOKEY POKEY

English folk song

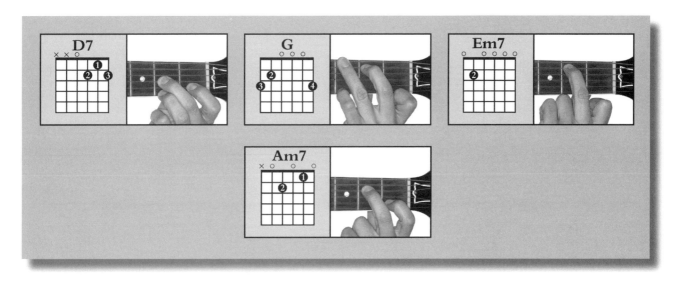

With a steady beat

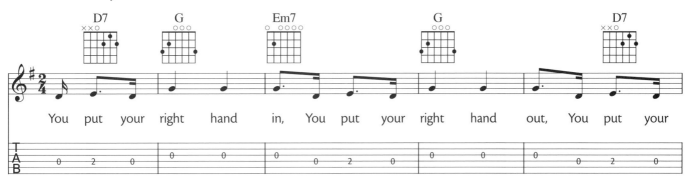

You put your right hand in, You put your right hand out, You put your

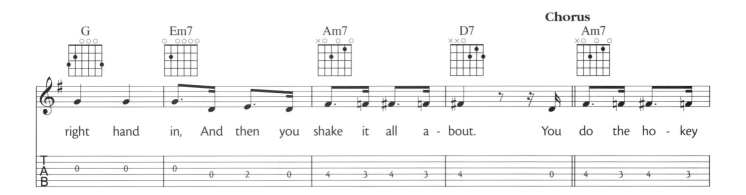

Chorus

right hand in, And then you shake it all a - bout. You do the ho - key

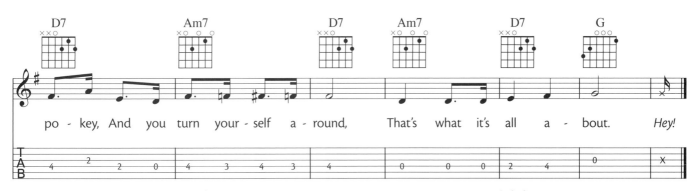

po - key, And you turn your - self a - round, That's what it's all a - bout. *Hey!*

2.. You put your left hand in, *etc.*

3. You put your right foot in, *etc.*

4. You put your left foot in, *etc.*

5. You put your whole self in, *etc.*

HOME ON THE RANGE

American cowboy song

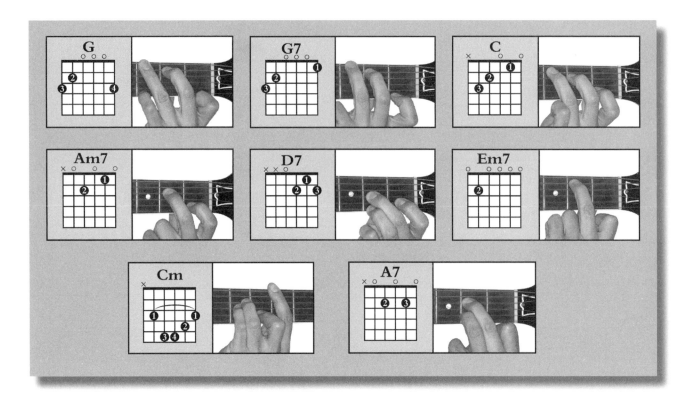

Moderately

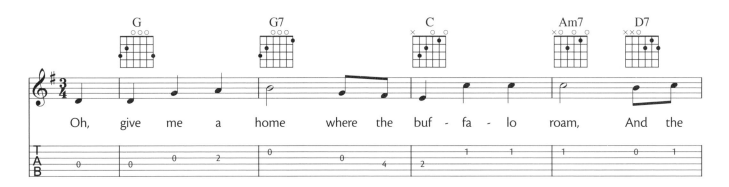

Oh, give me a home where the buf - fa - lo roam, And the

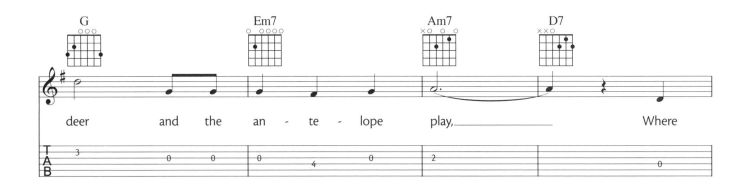

deer and the an - te - lope play,_____ Where

THE HOLLY AND THE IVY

English carol

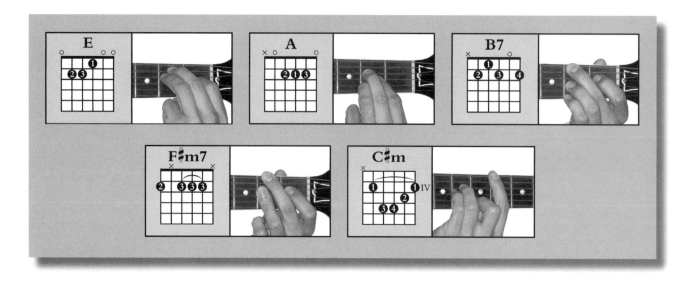

With feeling

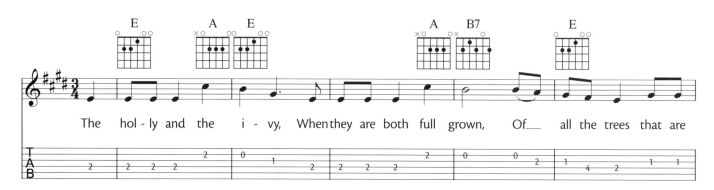

The hol-ly and the i-vy, When they are both full grown, Of__ all the trees that are

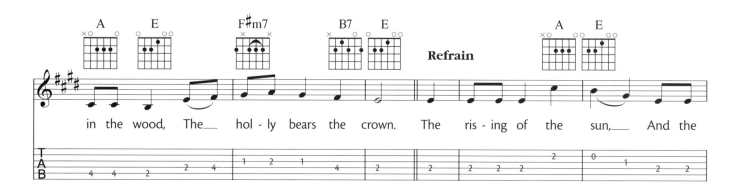

in the wood, The__ hol-ly bears the crown. The ris-ing of the sun,__ And the

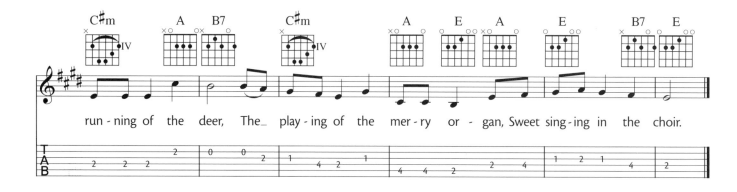

run-ning of the deer, The_ play-ing of the mer-ry or-gan, Sweet sing-ing in the choir.

HOT TIME IN THE OLD TOWN TONIGHT

Words by Joseph Hayden • Music by Theodore M. Metz

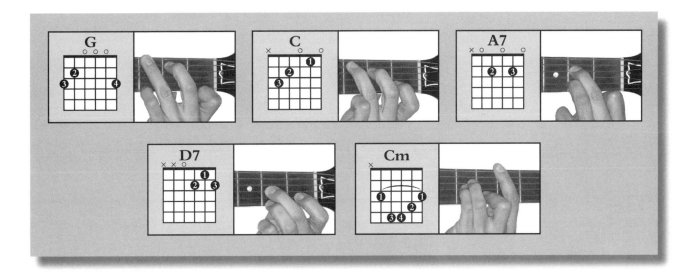

With a steady beat

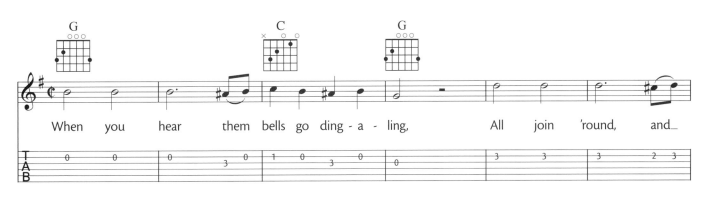

When you hear them bells go ding-a-ling, All join 'round, and

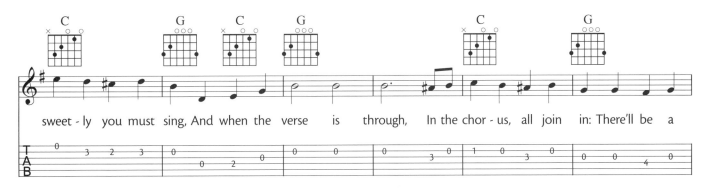

sweet-ly you must sing, And when the verse is through, In the chor-us, all join in: There'll be a

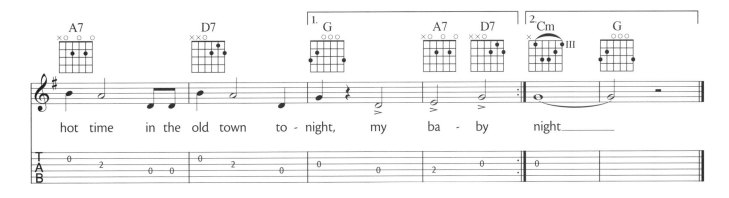

hot time in the old town to-night, my ba-by night____

HOUSE OF THE RISING SUN

American folk song

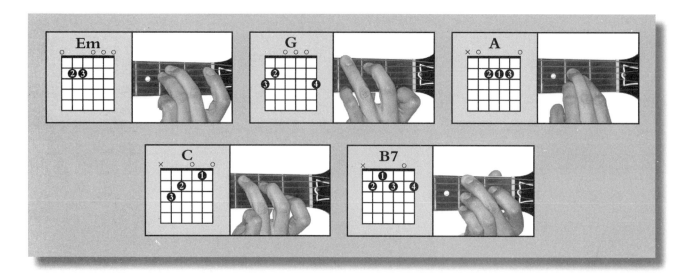

Moderately slow

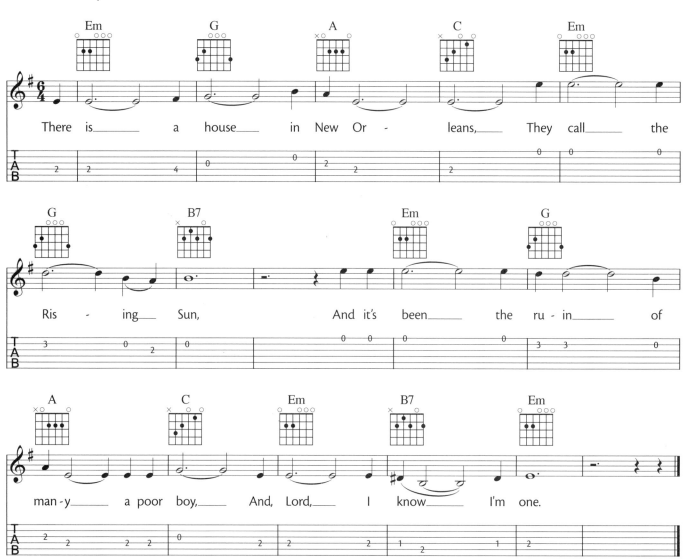

I KNOW WHERE I'M GOING

American folk song

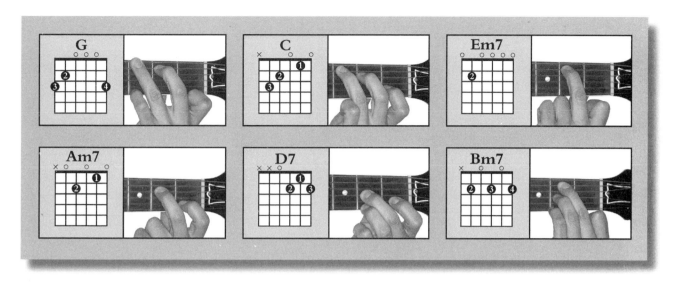

Freely

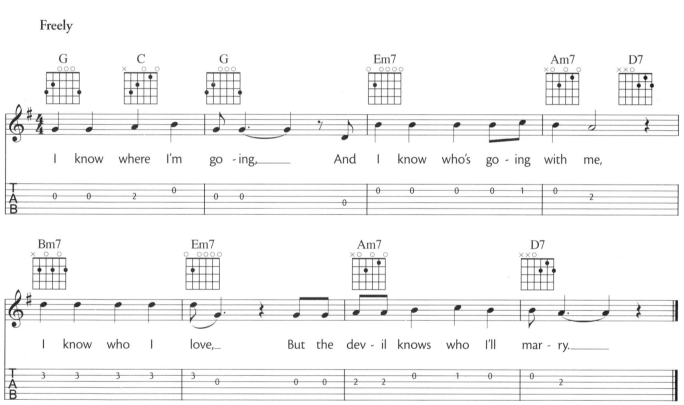

I know where I'm go-ing,___ And I know who's go-ing with me,

I know who I love,___ But the dev-il knows who I'll mar-ry.___

2.. Feather beds are soft,
And painted rooms are bonny
But I would trade them all,
To go with my love, Johnny.

3. Some say he's bad,
But I say he's bonny.
Fairest of them all
Is my handsome, winsome Johnny.

4. I know where I'm going,
And I know who's going with me,
I know who I love,
But the devil knows who I'll marry!

I AIN'T GOT NOBODY

Words by Roger Graham • Music by Spencer Williams & Dave Peyton

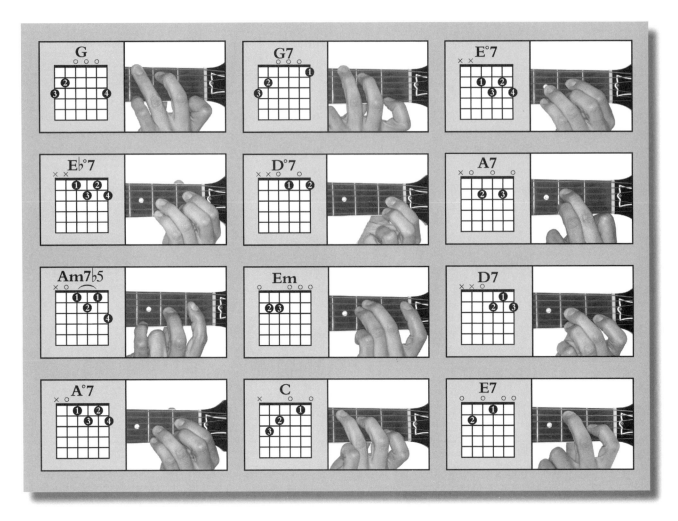

Moderately

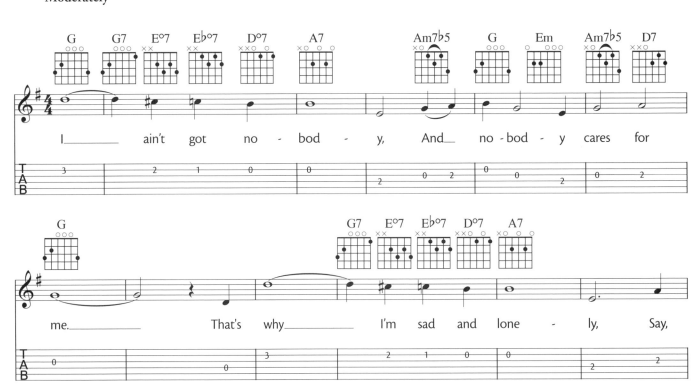

I LOVE YOU TRULY

Words and music by Carrie Jacobs-Bond

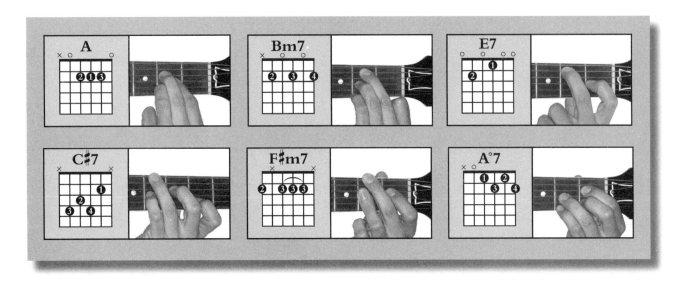

Tenderly

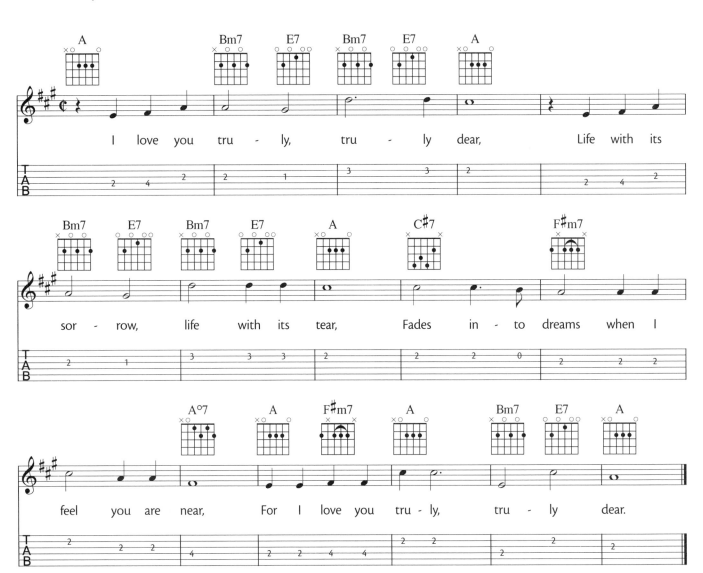

I love you tru - ly, tru - ly dear, Life with its

sor - row, life with its tear, Fades in - to dreams when I

feel you are near, For I love you tru - ly, tru - ly dear.

I'LL BUILD A STAIRWAY TO PARADISE

Words by B.G. DeSylva and Ira Gershwin • Music by George Gershwin

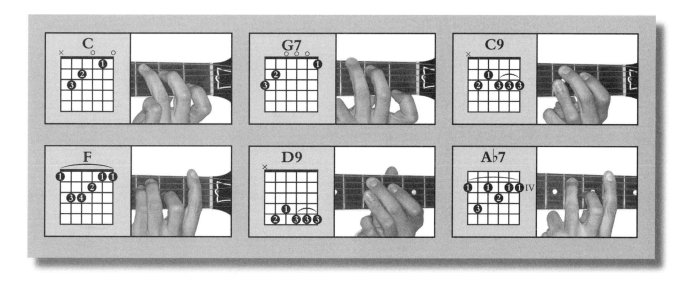

Moderately slow

I'll build a stair-way to par-a-dise, With a new step ev-'ry day! I'm going to get there at a-ny price, Stand a-side I'm on my way. I've got the blues___ And up a-bove it's so fair. Shoes! Go on and car-ry me there. I'll build a stair-way to par-a-dise, With a new step ev-'ry day.

I'M ALWAYS CHASING RAINBOWS

Words by Joseph McCarthy • Music by Harry Carroll

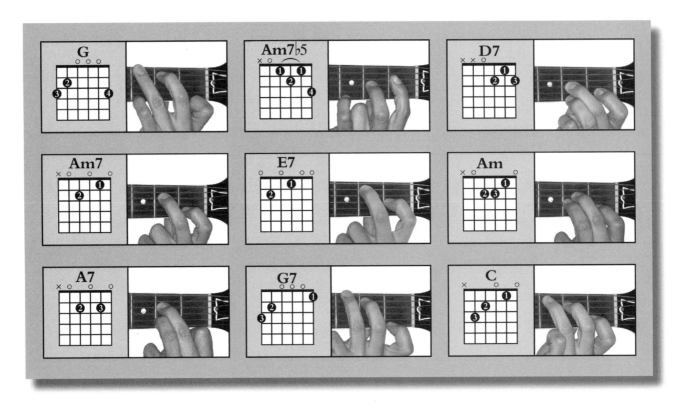

Slowly

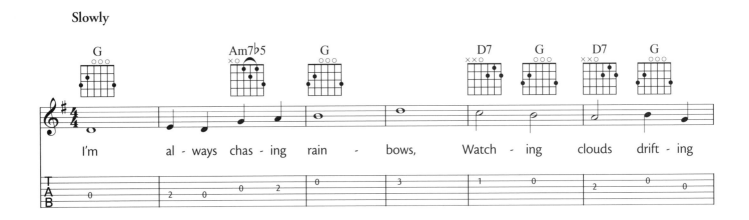

I'm al-ways chas-ing rain - bows, Watch - ing clouds drift - ing

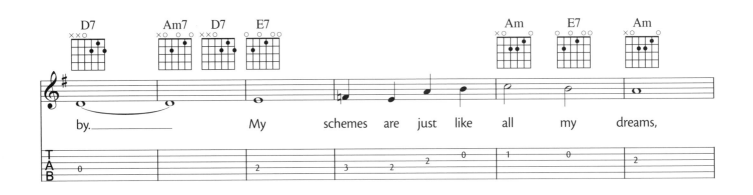

by._____ My schemes are just like all my dreams,

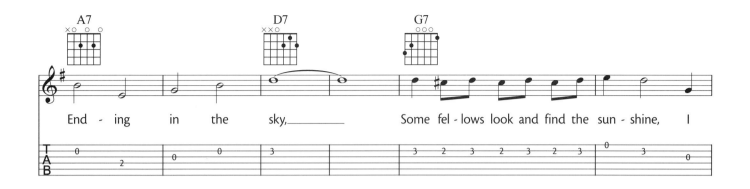

End - ing   in   the   sky,_____   Some fel - lows look and find the sun - shine,   I

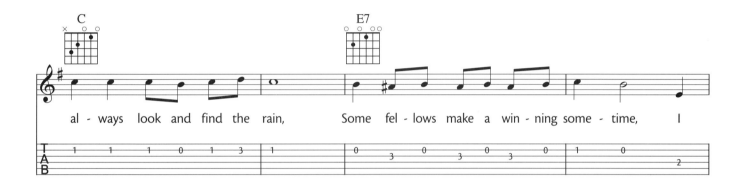

al - ways look and find the rain,   Some fel - lows make a win - ning some - time,   I

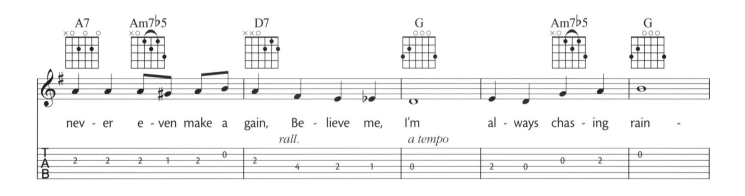

nev - er   e - ven make a gain,   Be - lieve me,   I'm   al - ways chas - ing rain -

rall.   *a tempo*

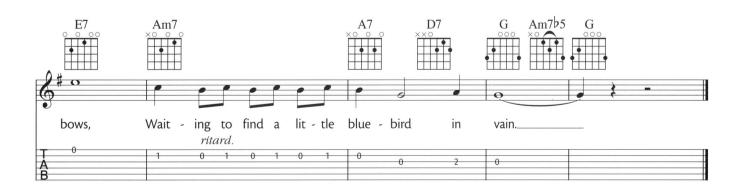

bows,   Wait - ing to find a lit - tle blue - bird   in   vain._____

ritard.

I'M JUST WILD ABOUT HARRY

Words by Noble Sissle • Music by Eubie Blake

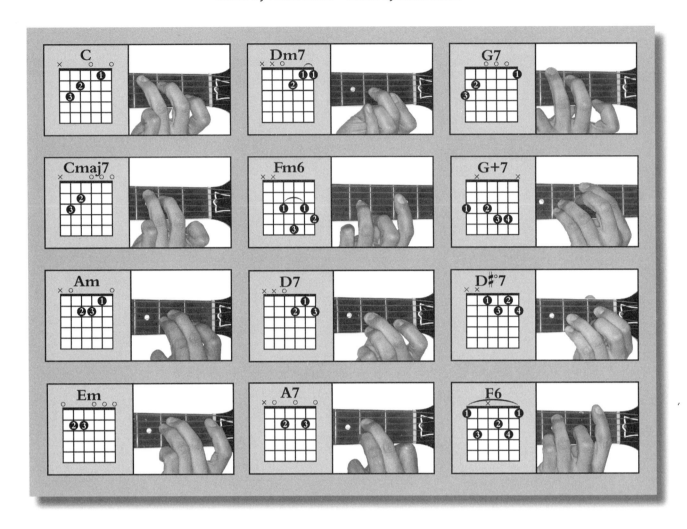

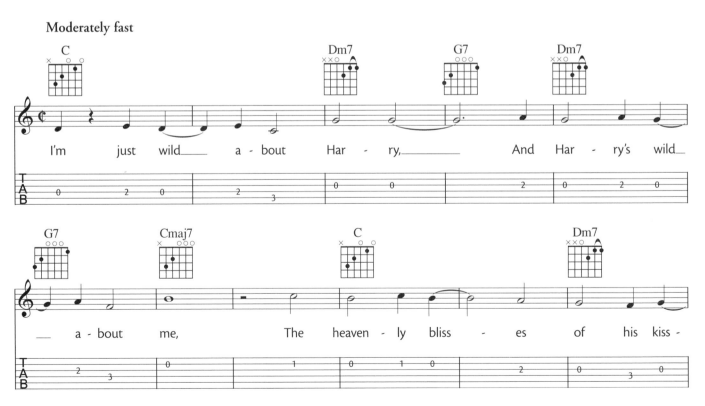

IN THE GOOD OLD SUMMERTIME

Words by Ren Shields • Music by George Evans

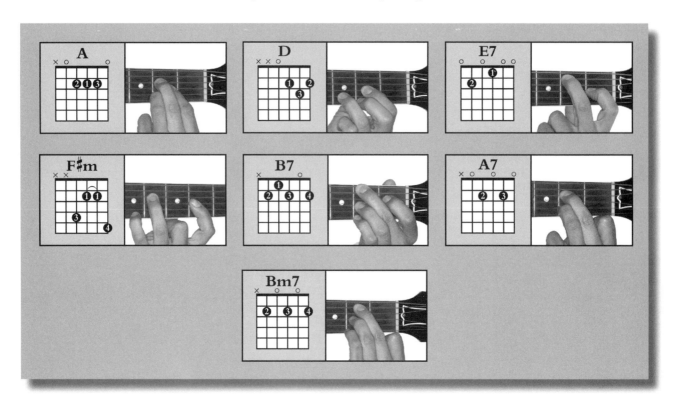

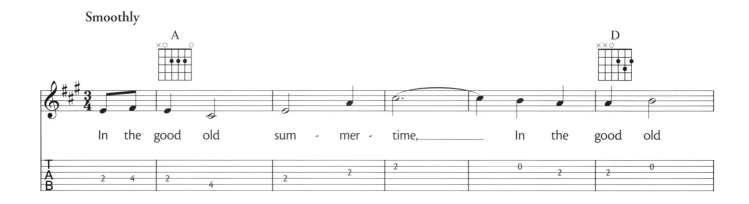

Smoothly

In the good old sum - mer - time,_____ In the good old

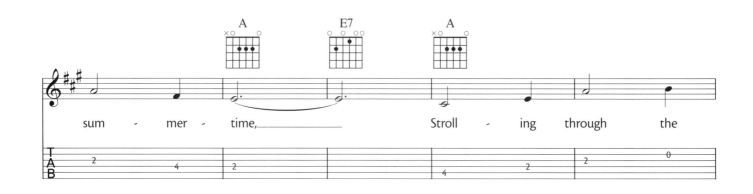

sum - mer - time,_____ Stroll - ing through the

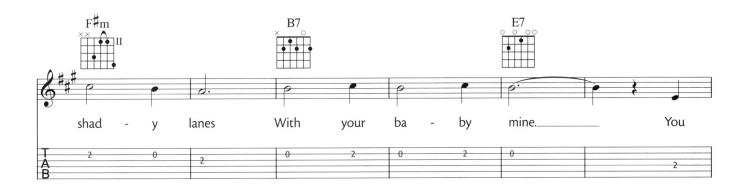

shad - y lanes   With   your   ba - by   mine._____   You

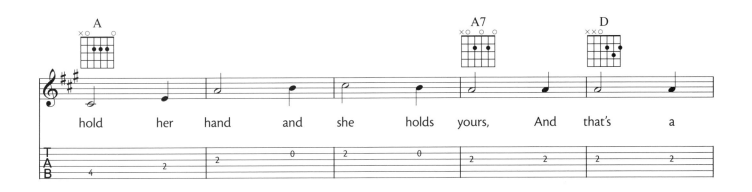

hold   her   hand   and   she   holds   yours,   And   that's   a

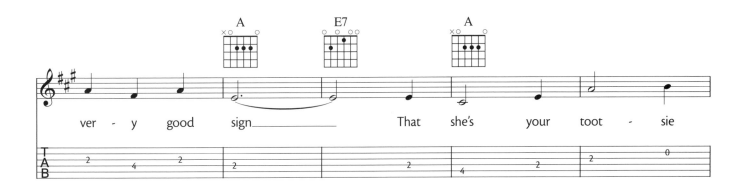

ver - y   good   sign_____   That   she's   your   toot - sie

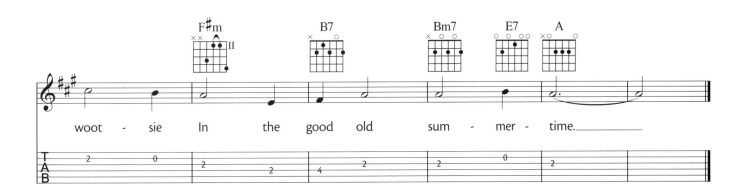

woot - sie   In   the   good   old   sum - mer - time._____

I WANT A GIRL

Words by William Dillon • Music by Harry Von Tilzer

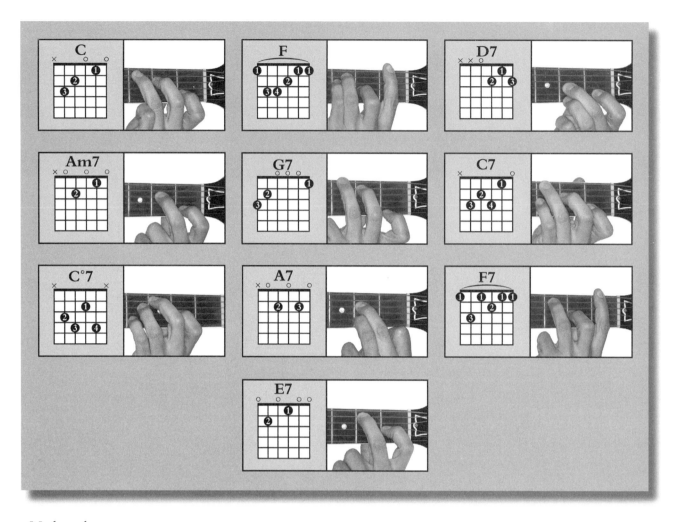

Moderately

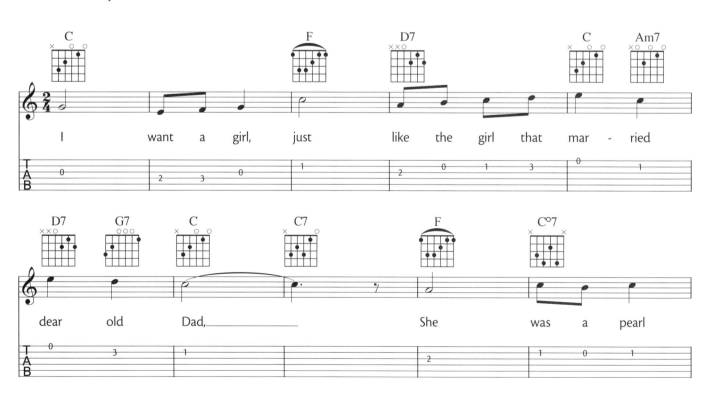

JA-DA

Words and music by Bob Carleton

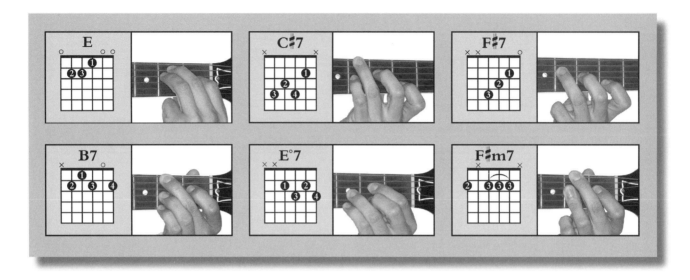

Moderately fast

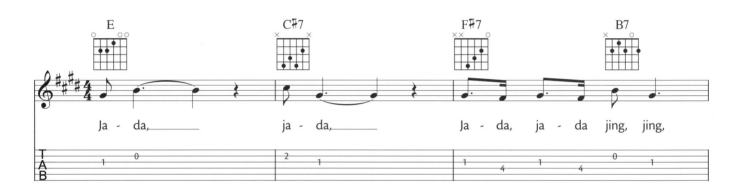

Ja - da,_____ ja - da,_____ Ja - da, ja - da jing, jing,

jing. Ja - da,_____ ja - da,_____

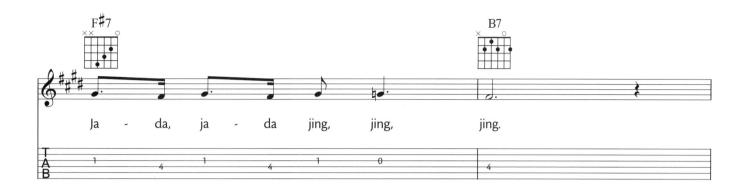

Ja - da, ja - da jing, jing, jing.

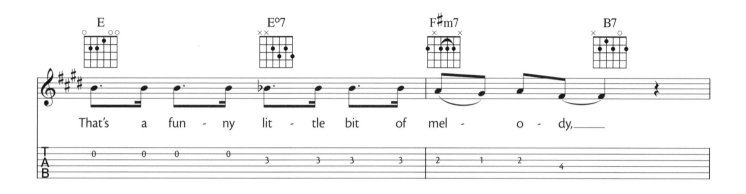

That's a fun - ny lit - tle bit of mel - o - dy,____

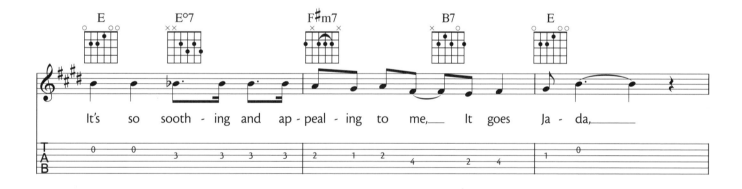

It's so sooth - ing and ap - peal - ing to me,____ It goes Ja - da,____

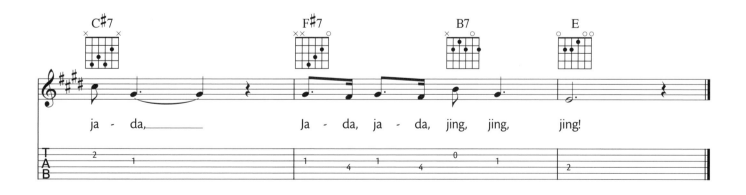

ja - da,____ Ja - da, ja - da, jing, jing, jing!

THE JAPANESE SANDMAN

Words by Raymond B. Egan • Music by Richard A. Whiting

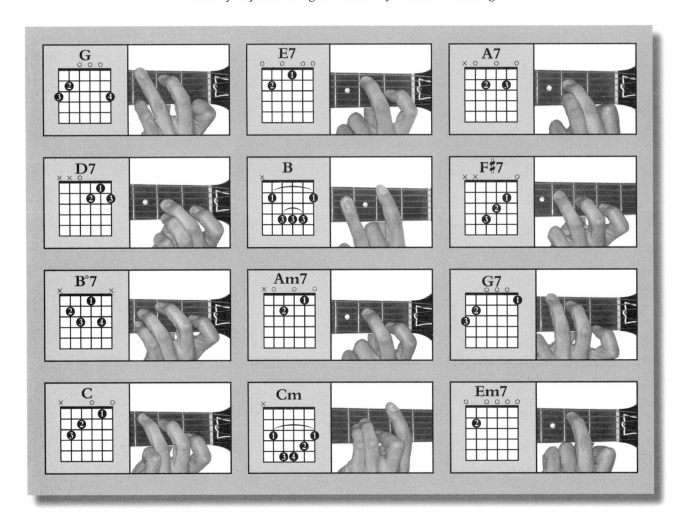

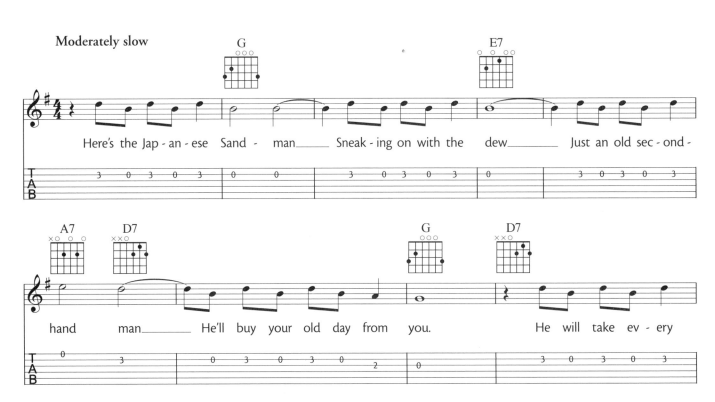

Moderately slow

Here's the Jap-an-ese Sand-man_____ Sneak-ing on with the dew_____ Just an old sec-ond-

hand man_____ He'll buy your old day from you. He will take ev-ery

JOHNNY HAS GONE FOR A SOLDIER

American folk song

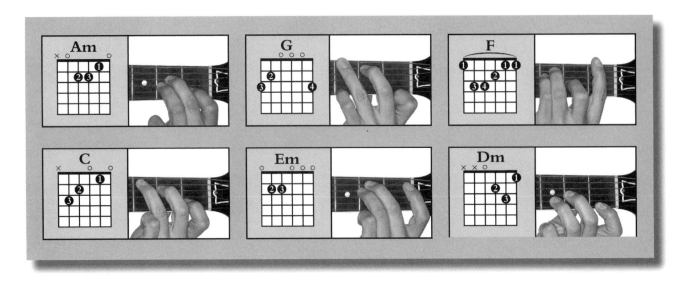

Slowly

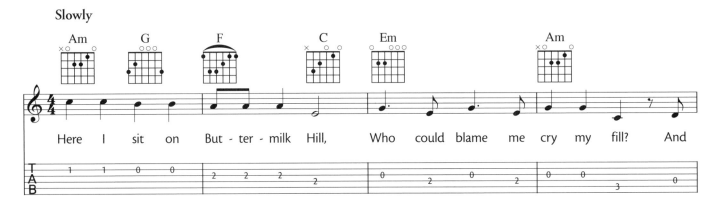

Here I sit on But-ter-milk Hill, Who could blame me cry my fill? And

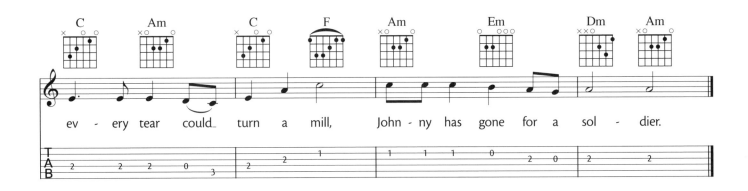

ev-ery tear could turn a mill, John-ny has gone for a sol-dier.

2.. I'll sell my clock, I'll sell my reel,
   Sell my little spinning wheel,
   To buy my love a sword of steel,
   Johnny has gone for a soldier.

3. Me, oh my, I love him so,
   Broke my heart to see him go,
   And only time can heal my woe,
   Johnny has gone for a soldier.

KEEP THE HOME FIRES BURNING

Words by Lena Guilbert Ford • Music by Ivor Novello

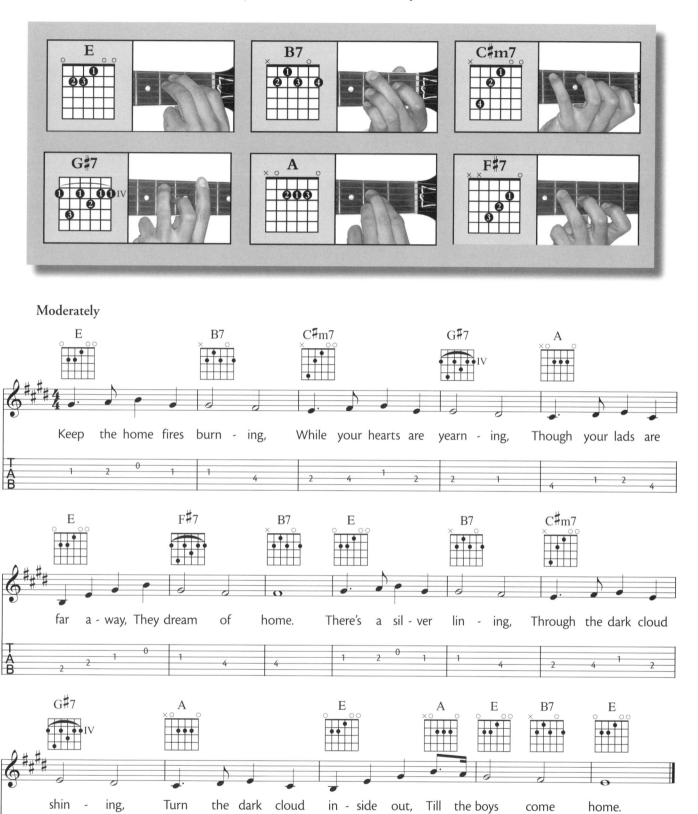

Moderately

Keep the home fires burn - ing, While your hearts are yearn - ing, Though your lads are far a - way, They dream of home. There's a sil - ver lin - ing, Through the dark cloud shin - ing, Turn the dark cloud in - side out, Till the boys come home.

KENTUCKY BABE

Words by Richard Buck • Music by Adam Geibel

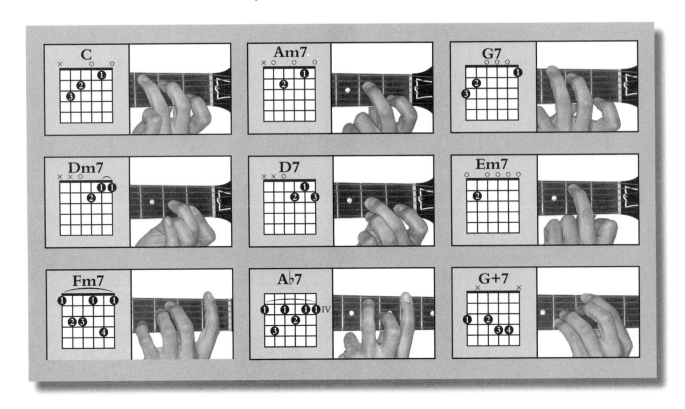

Moderately

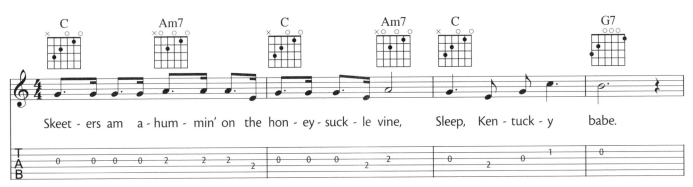

Skeet - ers am a - hum - min' on the hon - ey - suck - le vine, Sleep, Ken - tuck - y babe.

Sand - man am a - com - in' to this lit - tle babe of mine, Sleep, Ken - tuck - y babe.

LET ME CALL YOU SWEETHEART

Words and music by Beth Slater Whitson & Leo Friedman

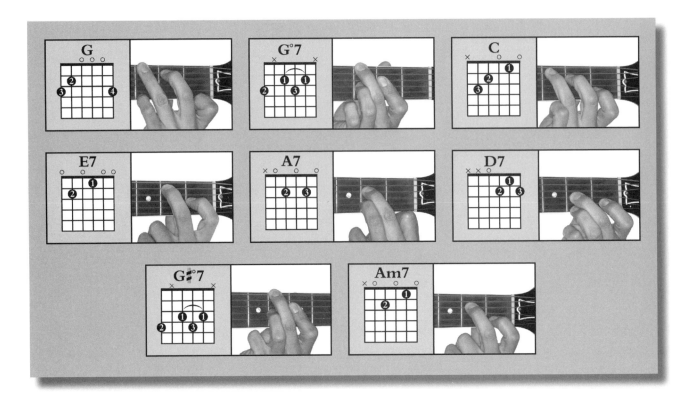

Slowly

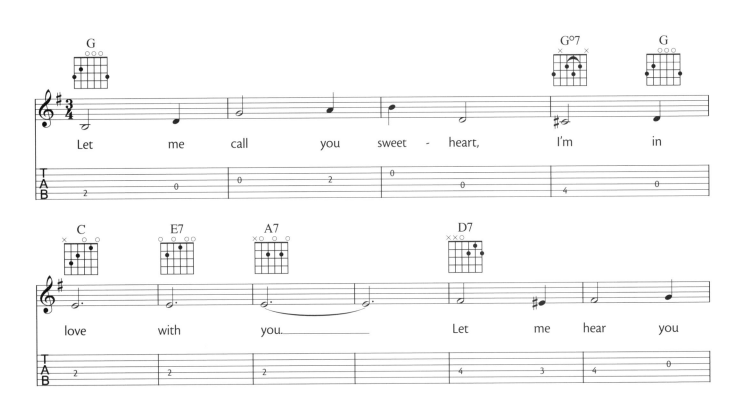

Let me call you sweet - heart, I'm in love with you._____ Let me hear you

LIMEHOUSE BLUES

Words by Douglas Furber • Music by Philip Braham

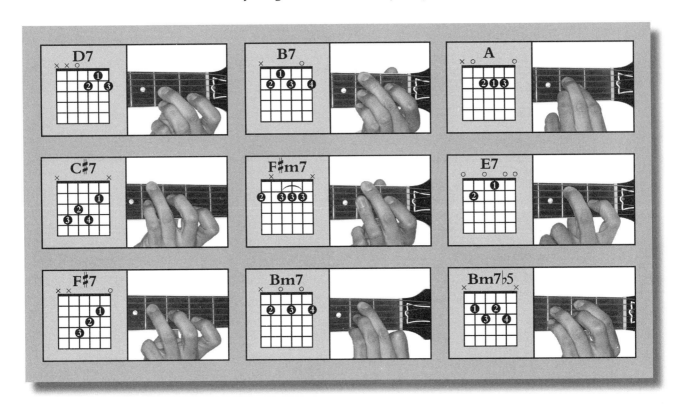

Moderately fast

Oh, Lime - house kid,_____ Oh, oh, oh, Lime - house kid,_____

Go - ing the way_____ that the rest of them did,_____

LOOK DOWN THAT LONESOME ROAD

American folk song

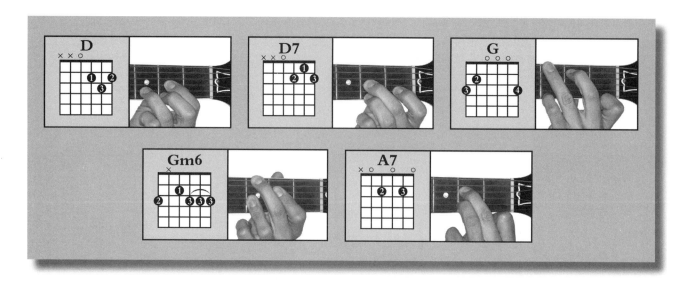

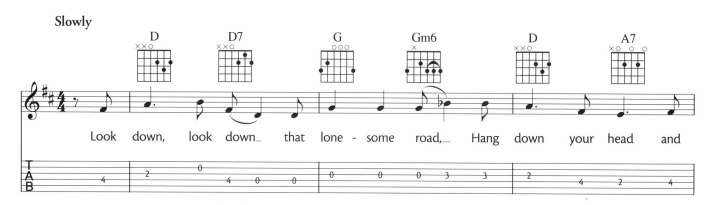

Slowly

Look down, look down_ that lone - some road,_ Hang down your head and

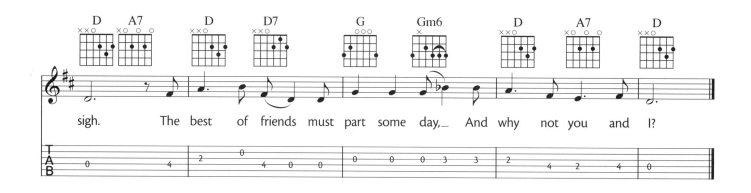

sigh. The best of friends must part some day,_ And why not you and I?

2. True love, true love, what have I done,
   That you should treat me so?
   You caused me to walk and talk with you,
   Like I never done before.

LULLY, LULLAY

English carol

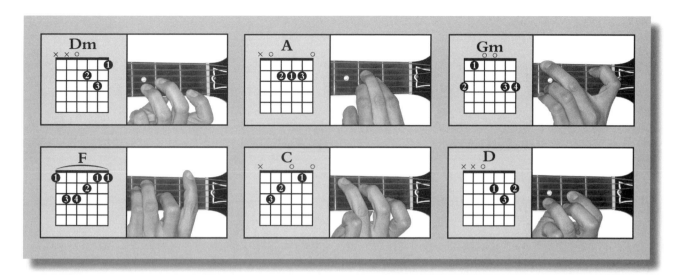

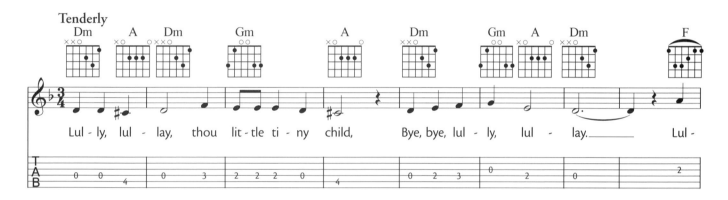

Tenderly

Lul - ly, lul - lay, thou lit - tle ti - ny child, Bye, bye, lul - ly, lul - lay._____ Lul -

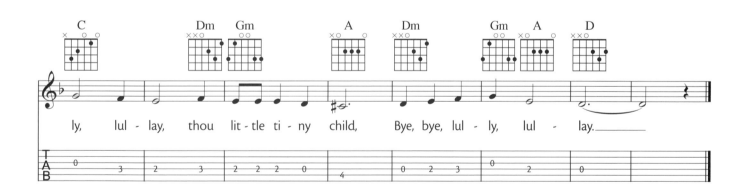

ly, lul - lay, thou lit - tle ti - ny child, Bye, bye, lul - ly, lul - lay._____

2.. Oh sisters too, how may we do,
    For to preserve this day;
    This poor youngling for whom we do sing:
    "Bye, bye, lully, lullay."

3. Herod the King in his raging
   Chargèd he hath this day
   His men of might in his own sight
   All young children to slay.

4. That woe is me, poor Child, for Thee,
   And ever mourn and pray
   For Thy parting, neither say nor sing:
   "Bye, bye, lully, lullay."

MEMORIES

Words by Gustave Kahn • Music by Egbert Van Alstyne

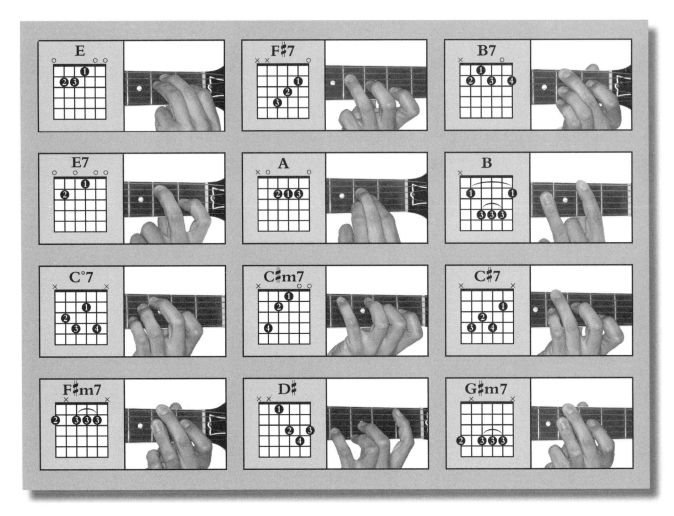

Moderately slow

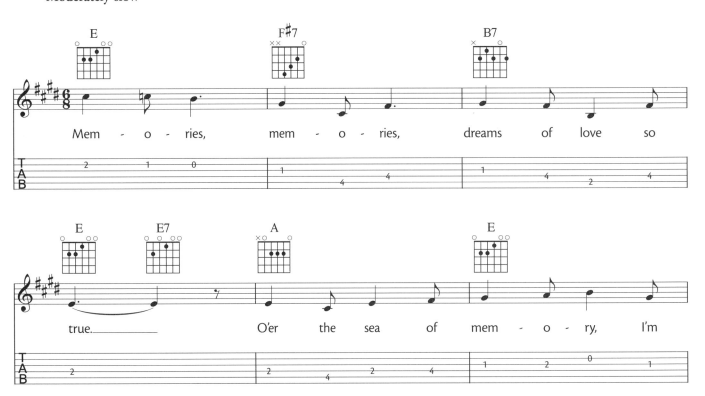

Mem - o - ries, mem - o - ries, dreams of love so

true.____ O'er the sea of mem - o - ry, I'm

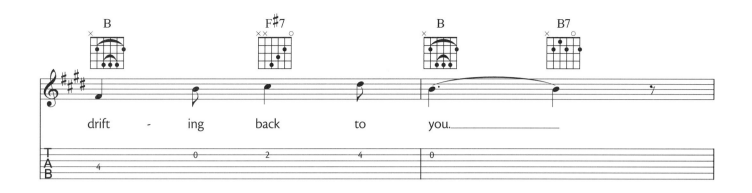

drift - ing back to you._____

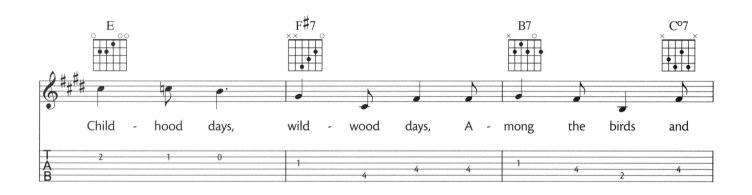

Child - hood days, wild - wood days, A - mong the birds and

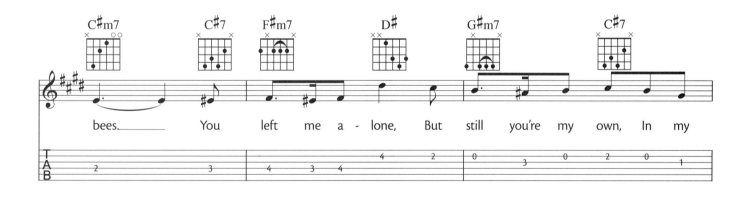

bees._____ You left me a - lone, But still you're my own, In my

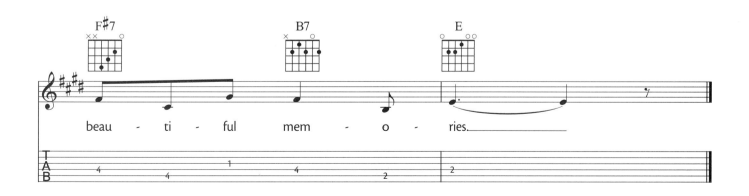

beau - ti - ful mem - o - ries._____

MICHAEL, ROW THE BOAT ASHORE

American folk song

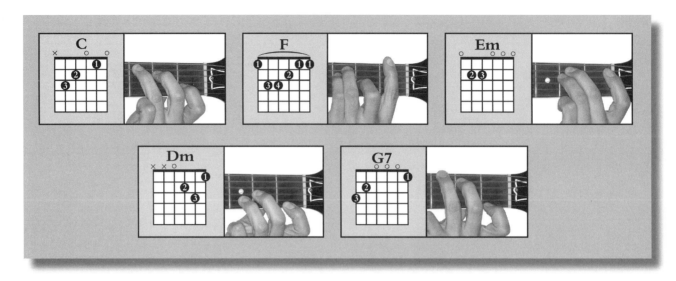

With spirit

Mi - chael, row the boat a - shore, Hal - le - lu - jah, Mi - chael, row the boat a -

shore, Hal - le - lu - jah. Sis - ter help to trim the sail, Hal - le -

lu - jah. Sis - ter help to trim the sail, Hal - le - lu - jah.

2. Jordan River is chilly and cold, Hallelujah,
   Chills the body, but not the soul, Hallelujah.
   Jordan River is deep and wide, Hallelujah,
   Milk and honey on the other side, Hallelujah.

3. Michael's boat is a music boat, Hallelujah,
   Michael's boat is a music boat, Hallelujah.
   Michael, row the boat ashore, Hallelujah,
   Michael, row the boat ashore, Hallelujah.

THE MIDNIGHT SPECIAL

American folk song

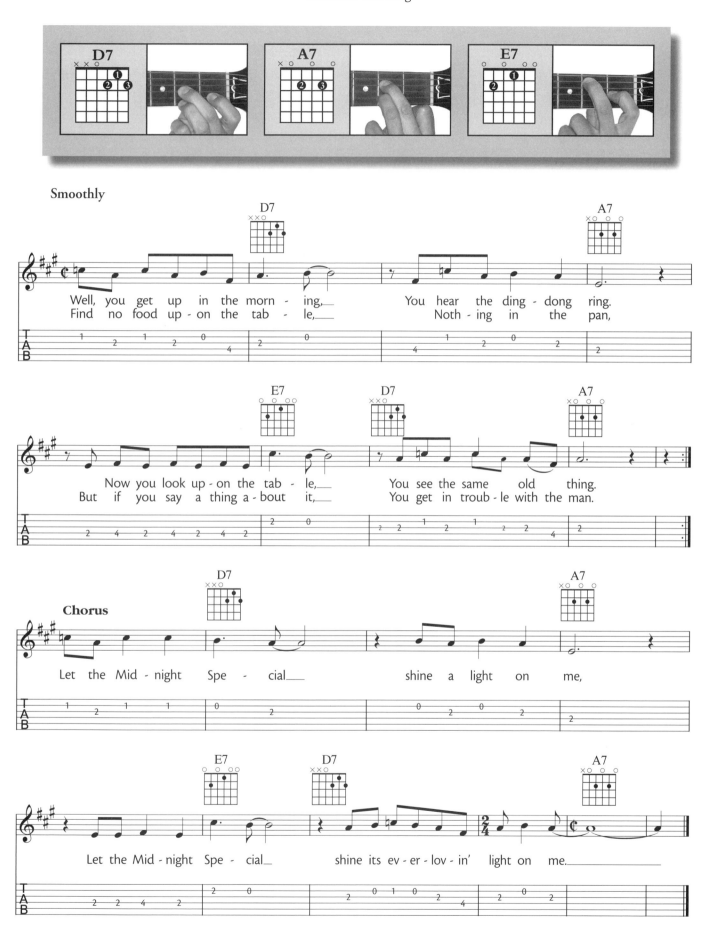

MOONLIGHT BAY

Words by Edward Madden • Music by Percy Wenrich

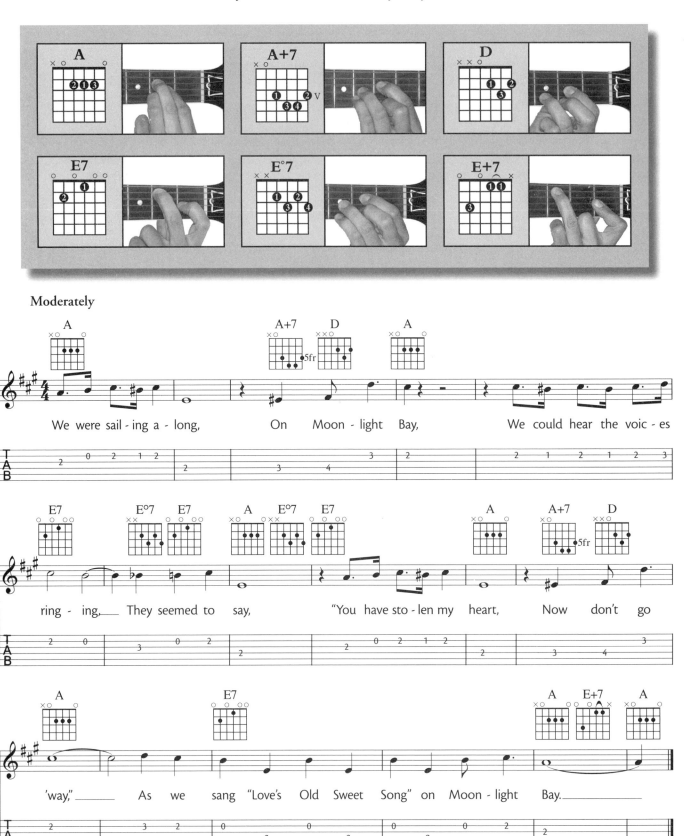

MORNING HAS BROKEN

American folk hymn

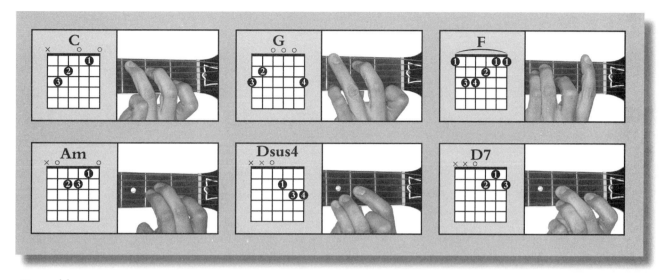

Smoothly

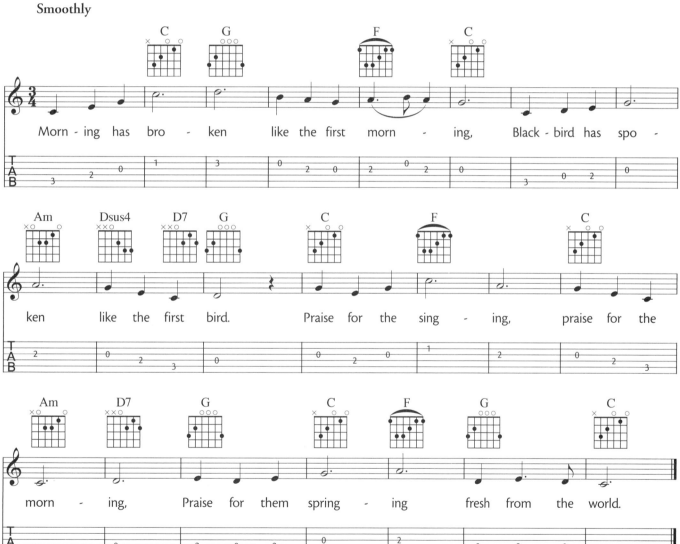

2. Sweet the rain's new fall, sunlit from heaven,
   Like the first dewfall on the first grass.
   Praise for the sweetness of the wet garden,
   Sprung in completeness where your feet pass.

3. Mine is the sunlight, mine is the morning,
   Born of the one light Eden saw play.
   Praise with elation, praise ev'ry morning,
   Each re-creation of the new day.

MOTHER

Words by Howard Johnson • Music by Theodore F. Morse

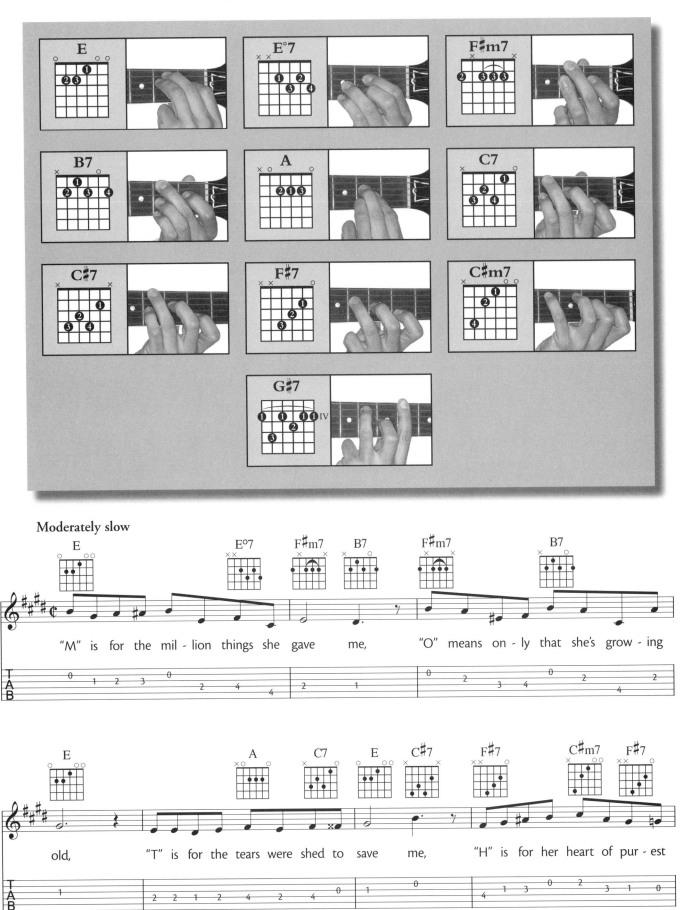

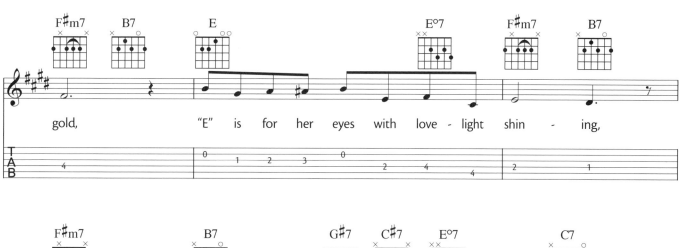

gold,   "E" is for her eyes with love - light shin - ing,

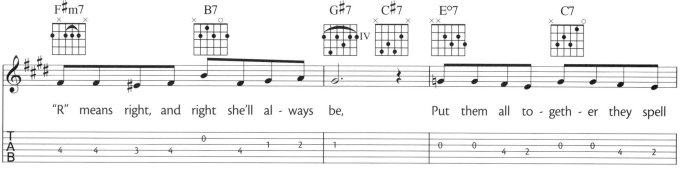

"R" means right, and right she'll al - ways be,   Put them all to - geth - er they spell

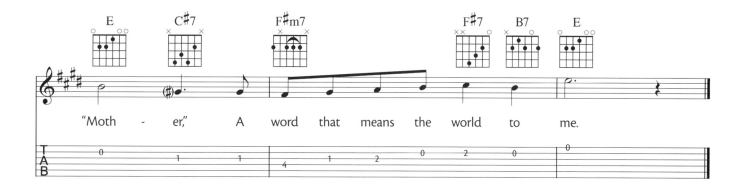

"Moth - er,"   A word that means the world to me.

2. "M" is for the mercy she possesses,
   "O" means that I owe her all I own,
   "T" is for her tender sweet caresses,
   "H" is for her hands that made a home;
   "E" means ev-'rything she's done to help me,
   "R" means real and regular, you see,
   Put them all together, they spell "Mother,"
   A word that means the world to me.

MY BUDDY

Words by Gus Kahn • Music by Walter Donaldson

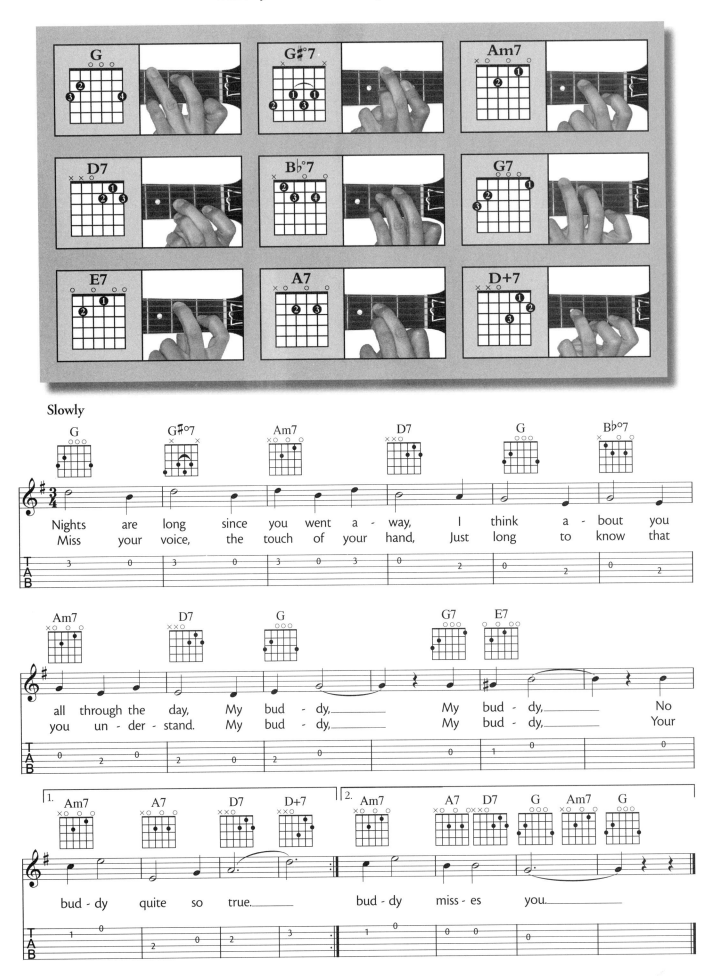

Nights are long, since you went a- way, I think a- bout you
Miss your voice, the touch of your hand, Just long to know you that

all through the day, My bud - dy, My bud - dy, No
you un- der- stand. My bud - dy, My bud - dy, Your

bud - dy quite so true. bud - dy miss - es you.

MY WILD IRISH ROSE

Words and music by Chauncey Olcott

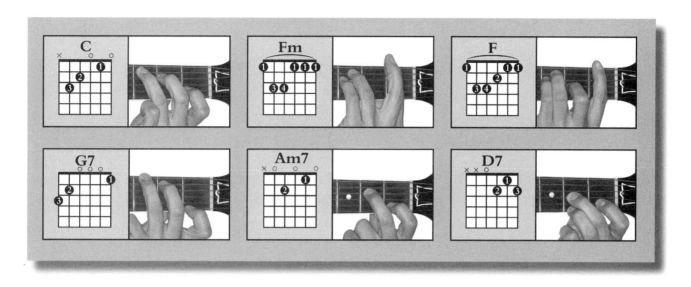

Moderately

My wild I - rish Rose,_____ The sweet - est flow'r that grows,_____ You may
My wild I - rish Rose,_____ The dear - est flow'r that grows,_____ And some

search ev - ery where, but none can com - pare With my wild I - rish
day for my sake, she may let me

1. Rose._____

2. take the bloom from my wild I - rish Rose._____

MY HONEY'S LOVIN' ARMS

Words by Herman Ruby • Music by Joseph Meyer

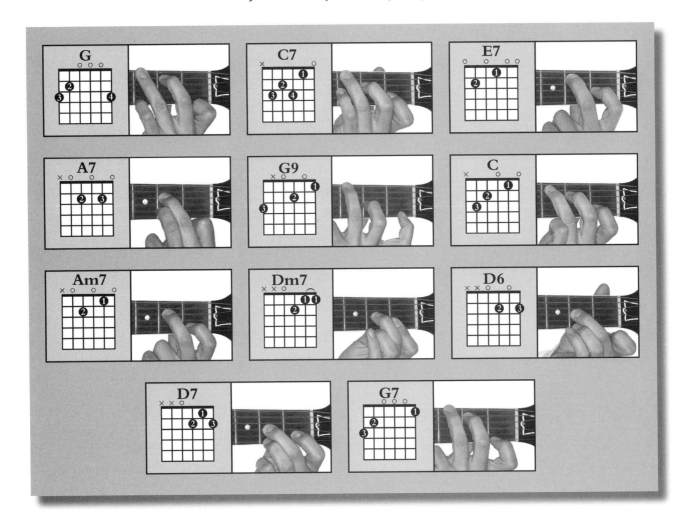

Moderately

I love your lov-in' arms,_ They hold a world of charms,

A place to nes-tle when I am lone - ly, A co-zy Mor-ris chair,

MY MELANCHOLY BABY

Words by George A. Nolan • Music by Ernie Burnett

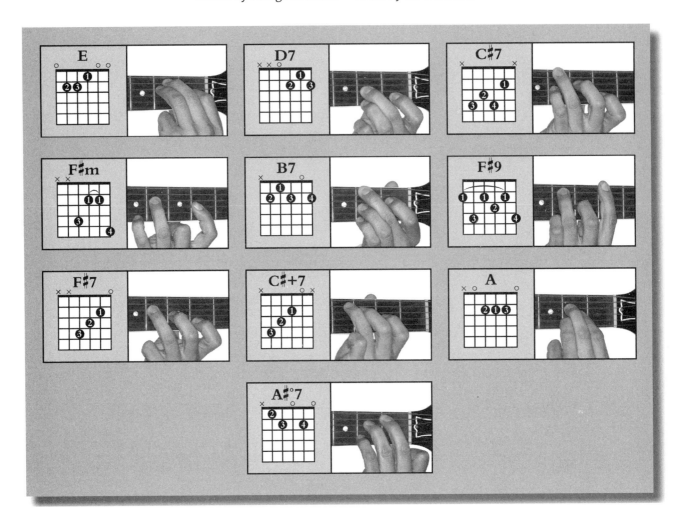

OH, HOW I HATE TO GET UP IN THE MORNING

Words and music by Irving Berlin

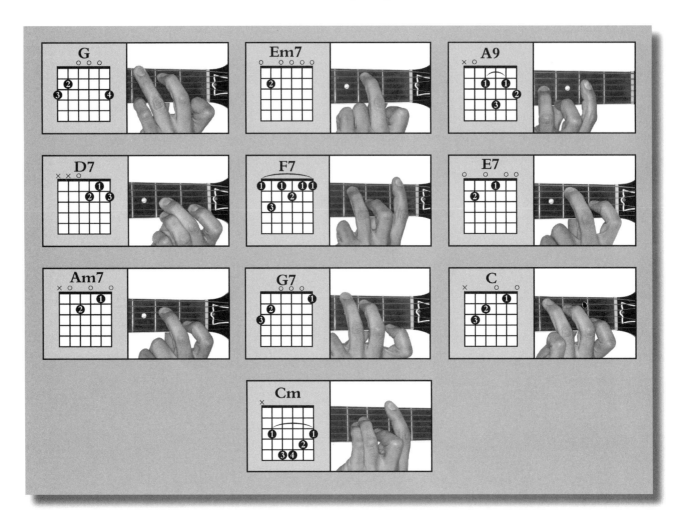

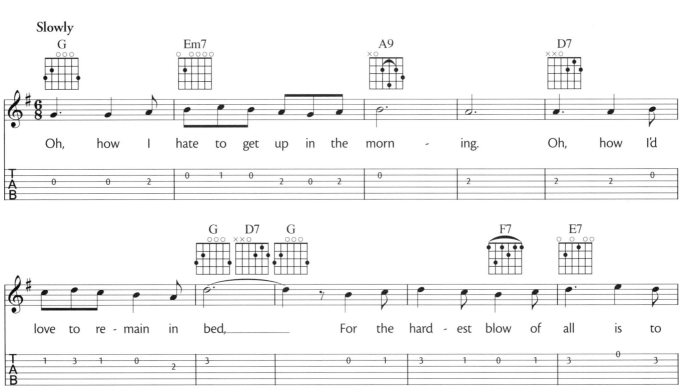

Slowly

Oh, how I hate to get up in the morn — ing. Oh, how I'd

love to re-main in bed,_____ For the hard-est blow of all is to

OH, CHRISTMAS TREE

German carol

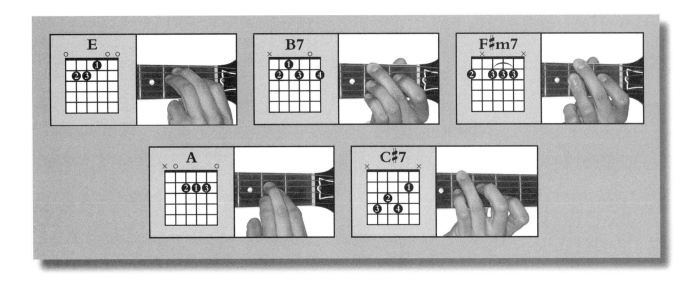

Smoothly

O Christ - mas tree, O Christ - mas tree, How true you stand un - chang - ing.

Your boughs so green in sum - mer - time, Re - main so green in win - ter - time. O

Christ - mas tree, O Christ - mas tree, How true you stand un - chang - ing.

OH, FREEDOM

American spiritual

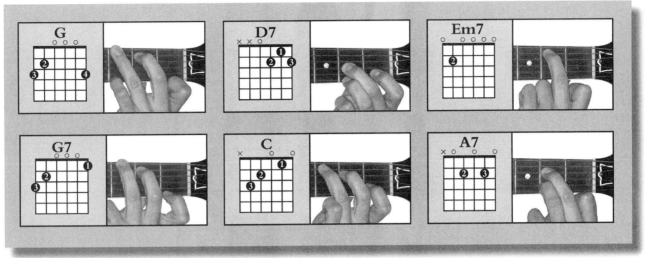

Freely

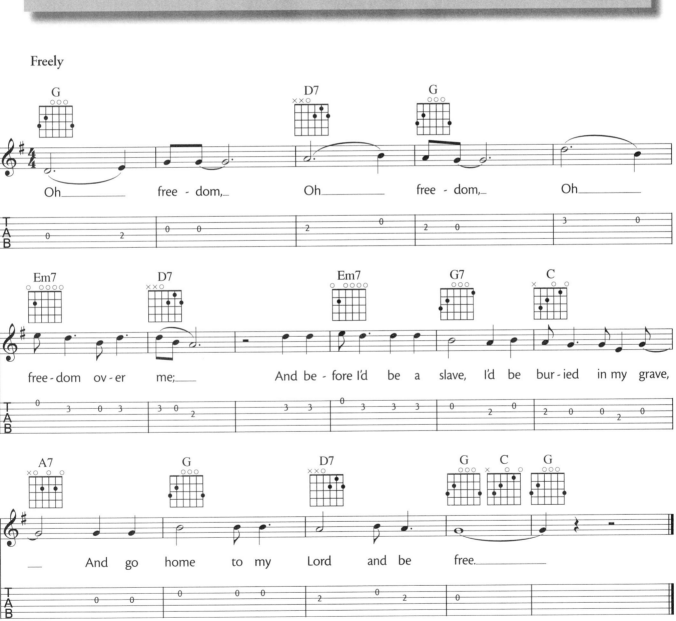

Oh free-dom,_ Oh____ free-dom,_ Oh____ free-dom ov-er me;____ And be-fore I'd be a slave, I'd be bur-ied in my grave, ____ And go home to my Lord and be free.____

OH, SUSANNA

Words and music by Stephen C. Foster

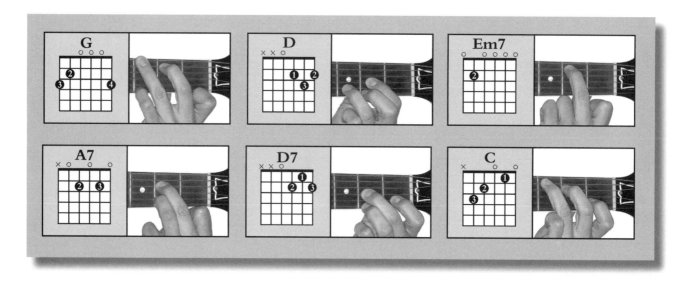

Moderately fast

OLD CHISHOLM TRAIL

American cowboy song

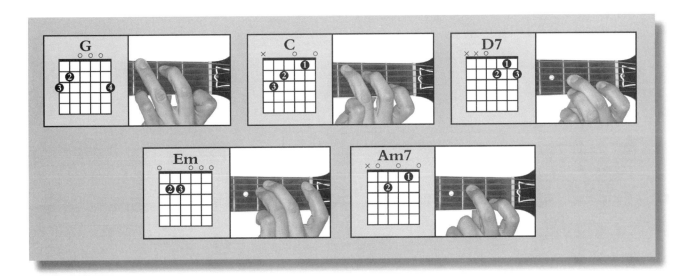

With energy

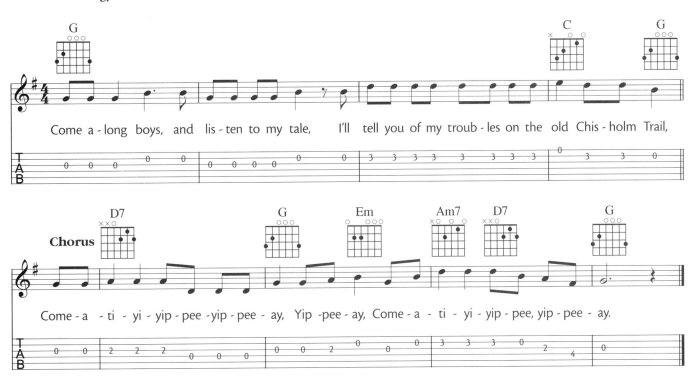

2. I woke up one morning on the Old Chisholm Trail,
   A rope in my hand and a cow by the tail.
   Chorus

3. A-roping and a-tying and a-branding all day,
   I'm working mighty hard for mighty little pay.
   Chorus

4. Saddle up boys and saddle up well,
   For I think these cattle have scattered to hell.
   Chorus

5. Make a circle, boys, don't lose no time,
   I'm sure that they'll be easy to find.
   Chorus

6. The wind begin to blow and the rain begin to fall,
   And it looked like we was going to lose them all.
   Chorus

7. Well I jumped in the saddle and grabbed the horn,
   Best darn cowboy ever was born.
   Chorus

8. So I went to the boss to draw my roll,
   And he had it figgered nine dollars in the hole.
   Chorus

9. Well I'll sell my saddle and I'll buy me a plow,
   And I swear I'll never rope another cow.
   Chorus

OLD FOLKS AT HOME

Words and music by Stephen C. Foster

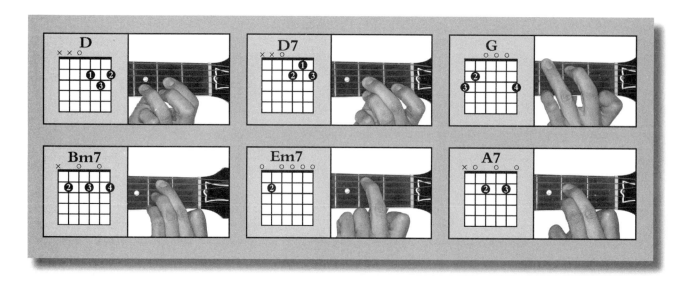

Smoothly

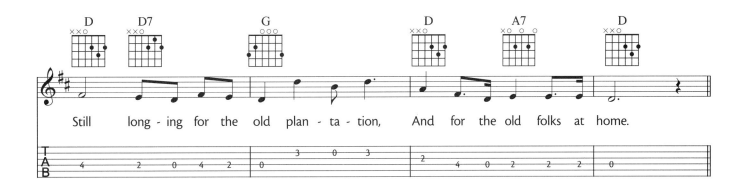

Still long-ing for the old plan-ta-tion, And for the old folks at home.

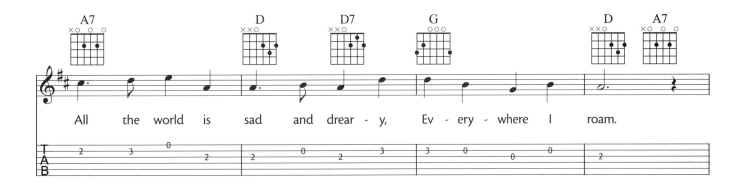

All the world is sad and drear-y, Ev-ery-where I roam.

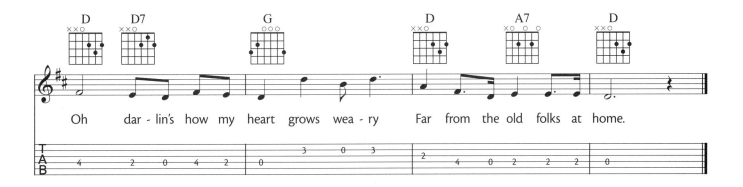

Oh dar-lin's how my heart grows wea-ry Far from the old folks at home.

2. All 'round the little farm I wandered
When I was young,
Then many happy days I squandered,
Many the songs I sung.
When I was playing with my brother,
Happy was I.
Oh! take me to my kind old mother,
There let me live and die.
Chorus

3. One little hut among the bushes
One that I love,
Still sadly to my mem'ry rushes,
No matter where I rove.
When will I see the bees a-humming,
All 'round the comb?
When will I hear the banjo strumming,
Down in my good old home?
Chorus

OVER THERE

Words and music by George M. Cohan

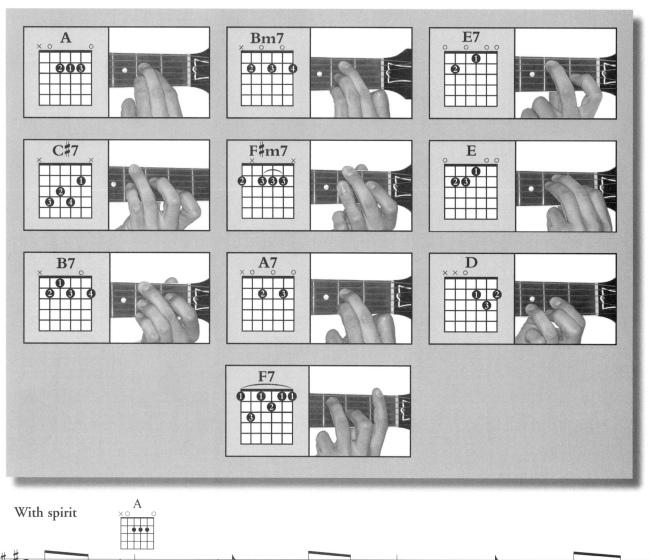

With spirit

O - ver there,_____ o - ver there,_____ send the

word, send the word o - ver there,_____ That the Yanks are

ON TOP OF OLD SMOKEY

American folk song

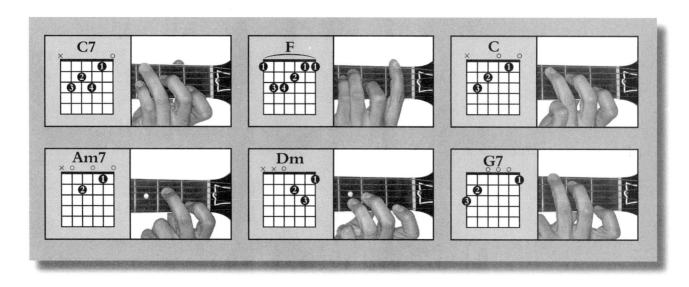

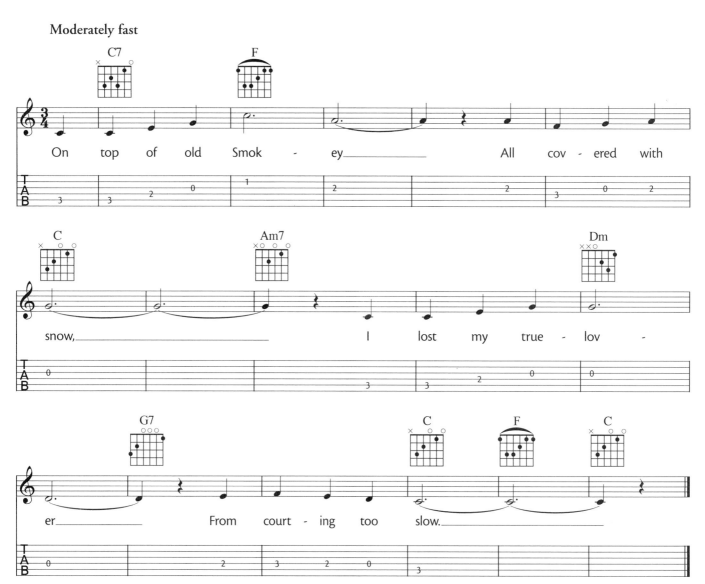

PLAY A SIMPLE MELODY

Words and music by Irving Berlin

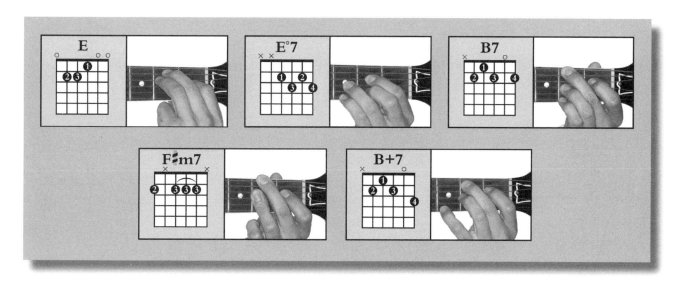

Moderately

Won't you play a simp - le mel - o - dy, Like my

moth - er sang to me? One with good old fash - ioned har - mo -

ny, Play a sim - ple mel - o - dy.

PAPER DOLL

Words and music by Johnny S. Black

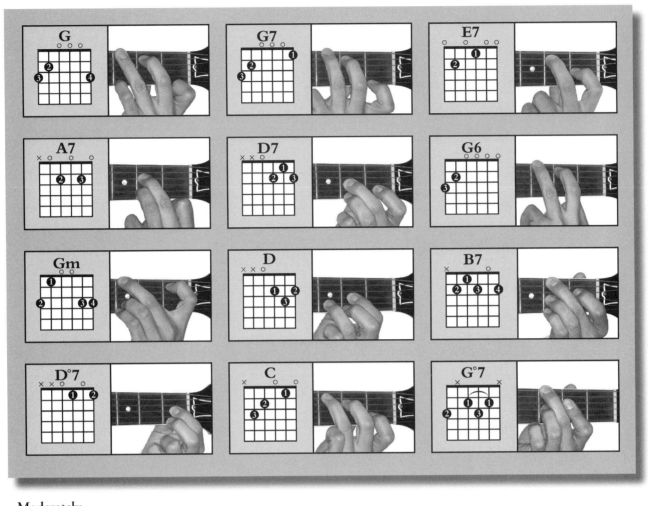

Moderately

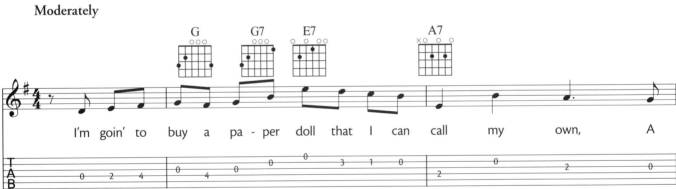

I'm goin' to buy a pa - per doll that I can call my own, A

doll that oth - er fel - lows can - not steal, And then the flir - ty, flir - ty guys, With their

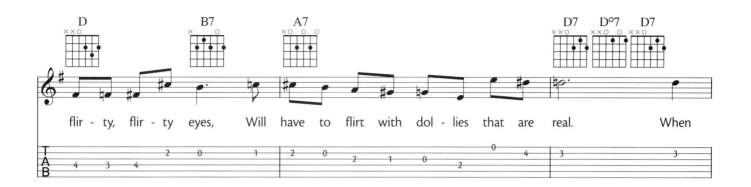

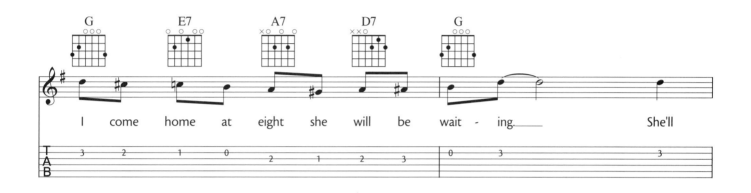

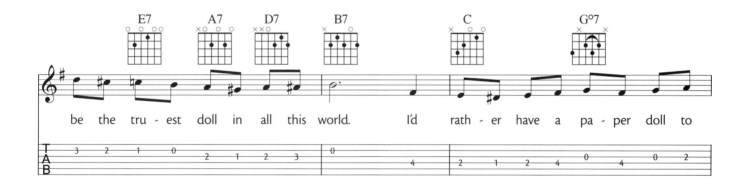

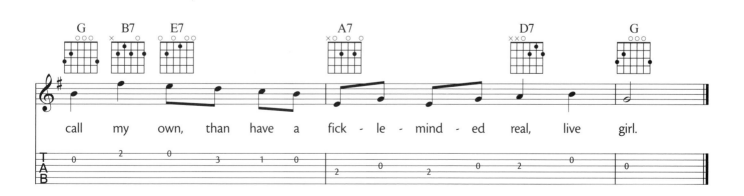

POOR BUTTERFLY

Words by John L. Golden • Music by Raymond Hubbell

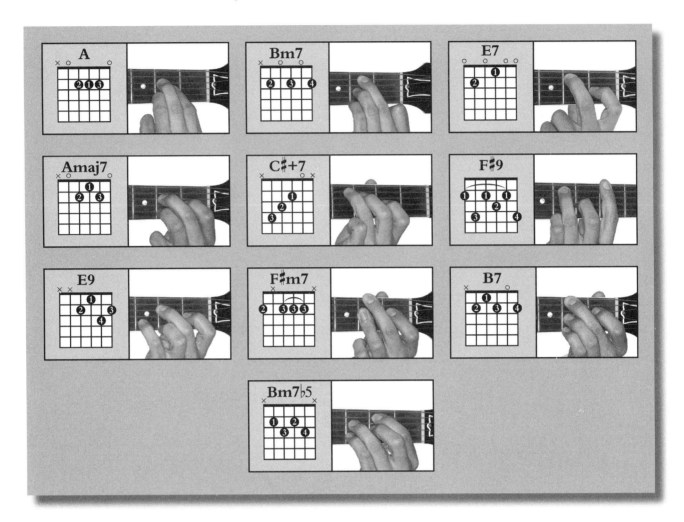

Slowly

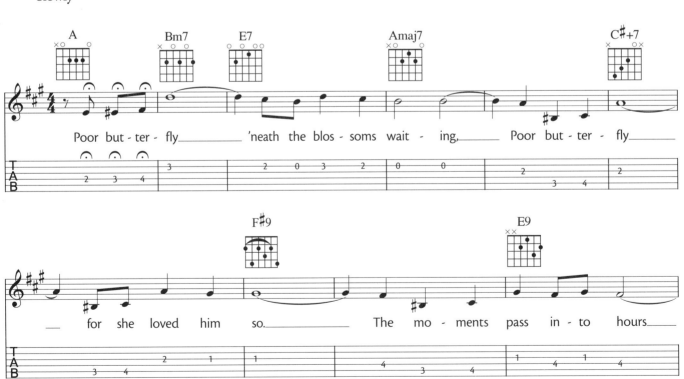

Poor but-ter-fly_____ 'neath the blos-soms wait - ing, Poor but-ter-fly_____

_____ for she loved him so._____ The mo - ments pass in - to hours_____

PRETTY BABY

Words by Gus Kahn • Music by Egbert Van Alstyne

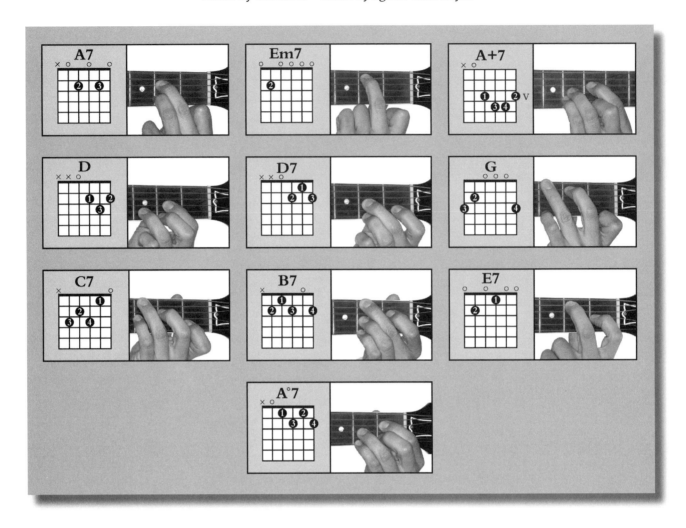

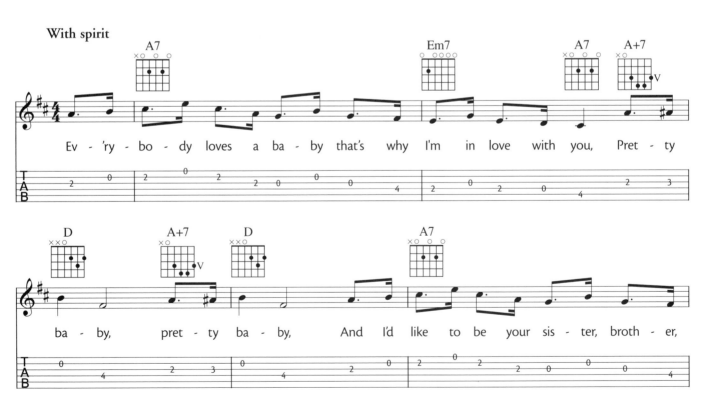

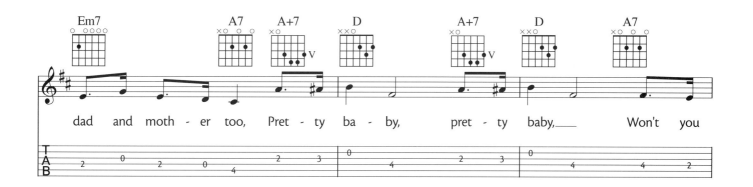

dad and moth - er too, Pret - ty ba - by, pret - ty baby,____ Won't you

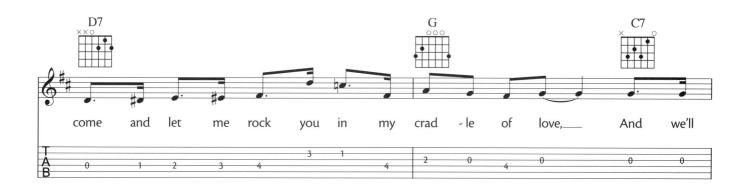

come and let me rock you in my crad - le of love,____ And we'll

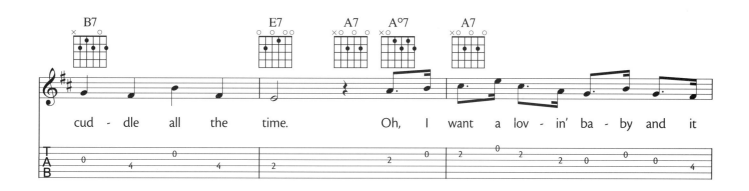

cud - dle all the time. Oh, I want a lov - in' ba - by and it

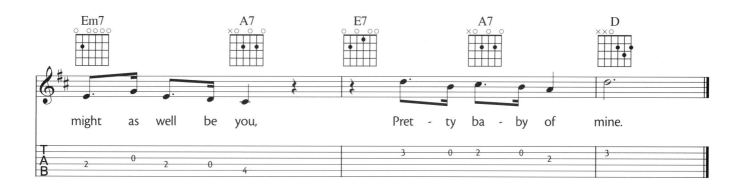

might as well be you, Pret - ty ba - by of mine.

A PRETTY GIRL IS LIKE A MELODY

Words and music by Irving Berlin

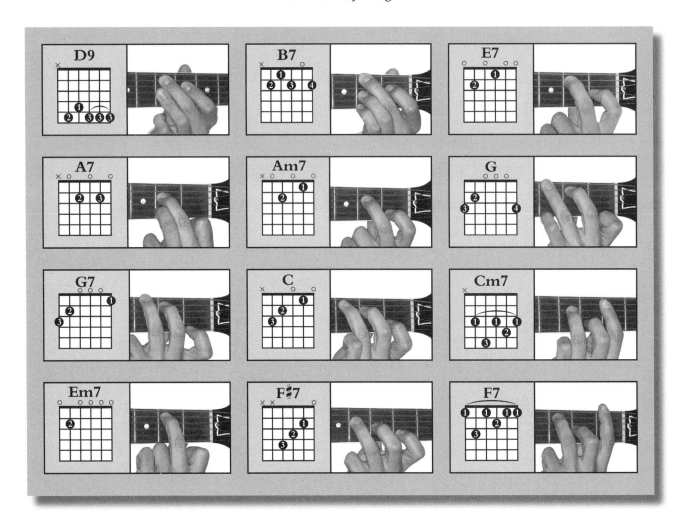

Moderately slow

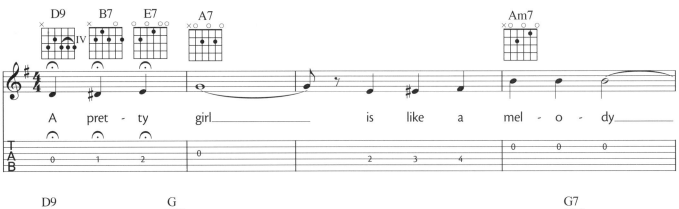

A pret - ty girl_____ is like a mel - o - dy_____

____ That haunts you night and day_____ Just like the

RAGTIME COWBOY JOE

Words and music by Lewis F. Muir, Grant Clarke & Maurice Abrahams

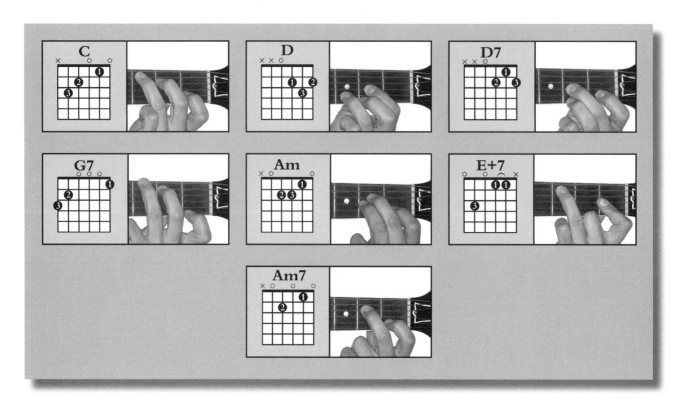

Smoothly

He al - ways sings rag - gy mu - sic to his cat - tle As he

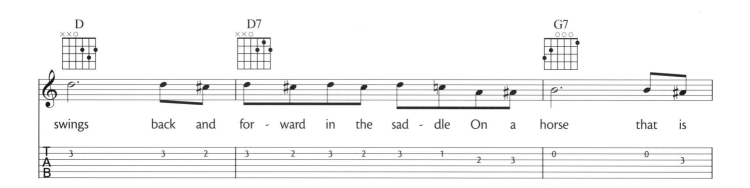

swings back and for - ward in the sad - dle On a horse that is

RED RIVER VALLEY

American cowboy song

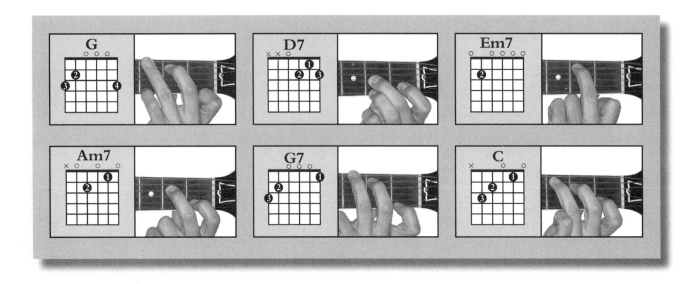

Smoothly

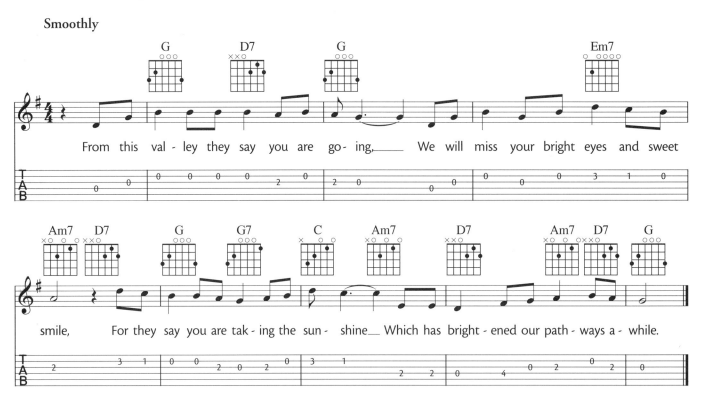

From this val - ley they say you are go - ing,____ We will miss your bright eyes and sweet

smile, For they say you are tak - ing the sun - shine____ Which has bright - ened our path - ways a - while.

2. Come and sit by my side, if you love me,
Do not hasten to bid me adieu,
Just remember the Red River Valley,
And the cowboy who loved you so true.

3. I've been thinking a long time, my darling,
Of the sweet words you never would say,
Now , alas, must my fond hopes all vanish?
For they say you are going away.

4. Do you think of the valley you're leaving?
Oh, how lonely and how dreary it will be.
Do you think of the kind hearts you're breaking,
And the pain you are causing to me?

5. They will bury me where you have wandered,
Near the hills where the daffodils grow,
When you're gone from the Red River Valley,
For I can't live without you I know.

THE RIDDLE SONG

American folk song

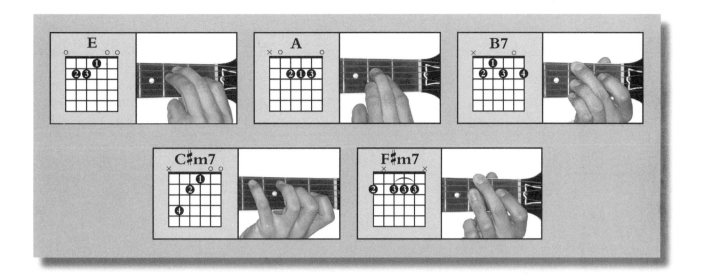

Moderately slow

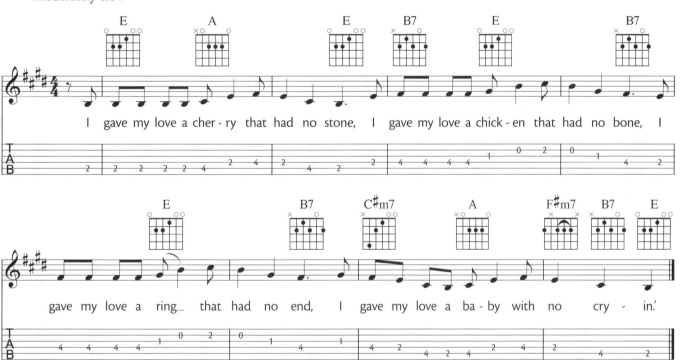

I gave my love a cher - ry that had no stone, I gave my love a chick - en that had no bone, I

gave my love a ring__ that had no end, I gave my love a ba - by with no cry - in.'

2. How can there be a cherry that has no stone?
   How can there be a chicken that has no bone?
   How can there be a ring that has no end?
   How can there be a baby with no cryin'?

3. A cherry when it's bloomin', it has no stone.
   A chicken when it's pippin', it has no bone.
   A ring when it's rollin', it has no end,
   A baby when it's sleepin' has no cryin'.

ROCK-A-BYE YOUR BABY WITH A DIXIE MELODY

Words by Sam M. Lewis & Joe Young • Music by Jean Schwartz

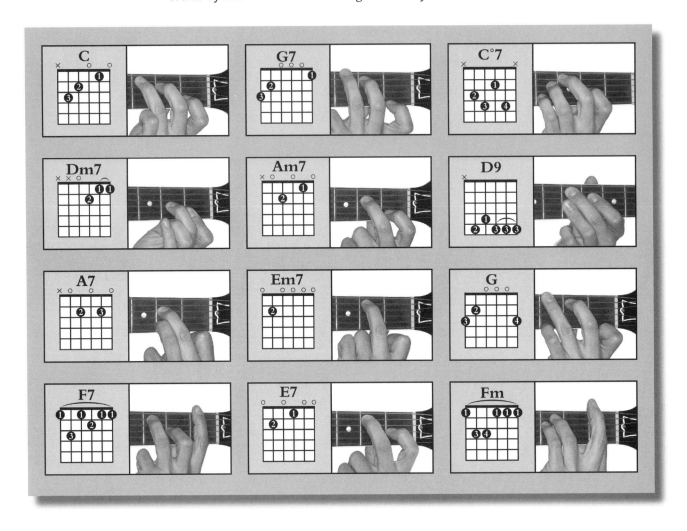

Moderately fast

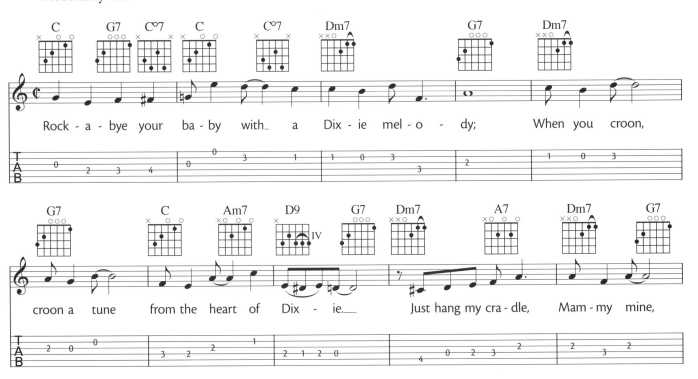

Rock - a - bye your ba - by with a Dix - ie mel - o - dy; When you croon,

croon a tune from the heart of Dix - ie. Just hang my cra - dle, Mam - my mine,

ROCK ISLAND LINE

American folk song

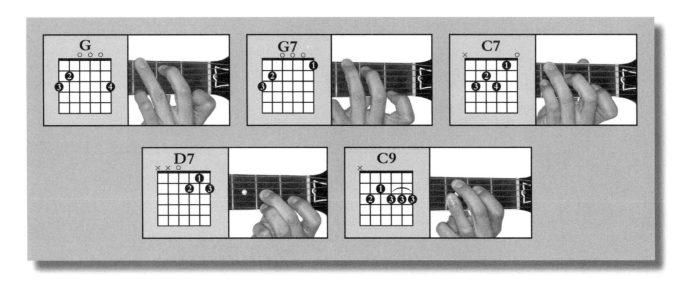

With spirit

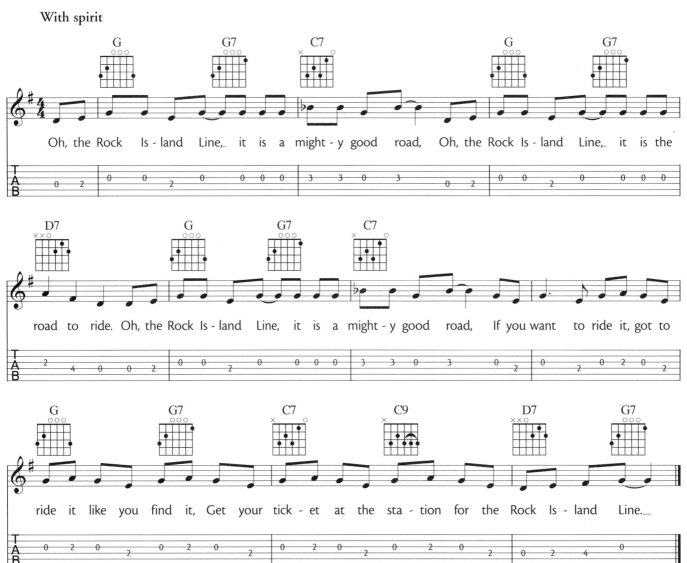

Oh, the Rock Is - land Line,_ it is a might - y good road, Oh, the Rock Is - land Line,_ it is the

road to ride. Oh, the Rock Is - land Line, it is a might - y good road, If you want to ride it, got to

ride it like you find it, Get your tick - et at the sta - tion for the Rock Is - land Line._

SCARBOROUGH FAIR

English folk song

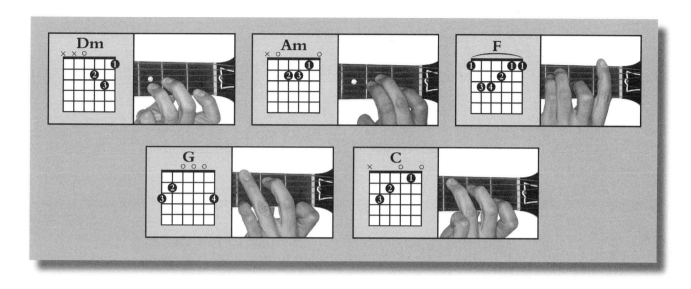

Moderately

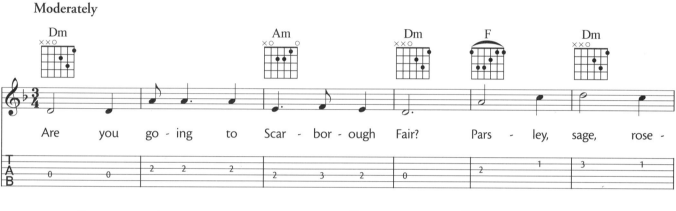

Are you go - ing to Scar - bor - ough Fair? Pars - ley, sage, rose -

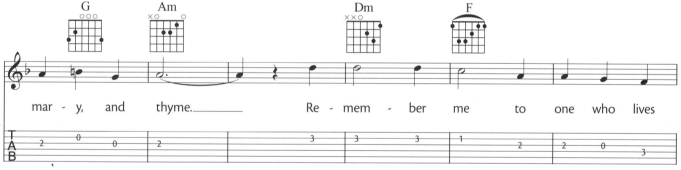

mar - y, and thyme.___ Re - mem - ber me to one who lives

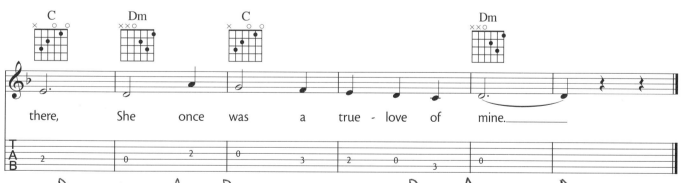

there, She once was a true - love of mine.___

2. Tell her to make me a cambric shirt,
Parsley, sage, rosemary, and thyme;
Without a seam or fine needlework,
And then she'll be a true love of mine.

3. Oh, will you find me an acre of land,
Parsley, sage, rosemary, and thyme;
Between the sea foam and the sea sand,
Or never be a true love of mine?

ST. LOUIS BLUES

Words and music by W.C. Handy

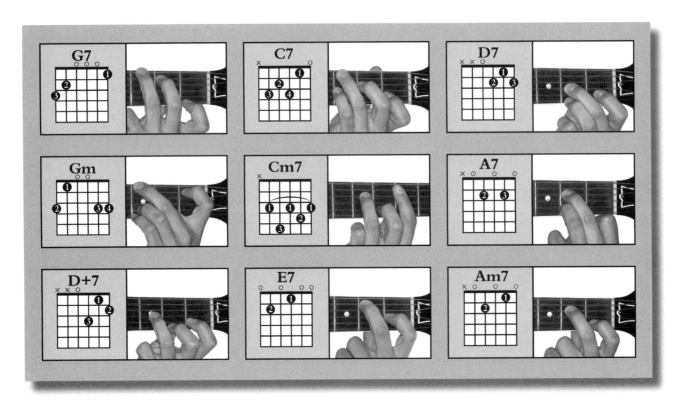

Freely

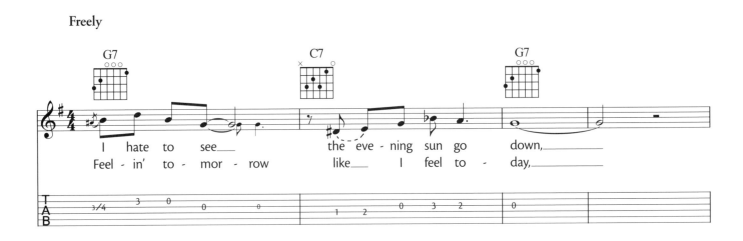

I hate to see___ the eve-ning sun go down,___
Feel-in' to-mor-row like___ I feel to-day,___

Hate to see___ the eve-ning sun go down,___
Feel to-mor-row like___ I feel to-day,___

SECOND HAND ROSE

Words by Grant Clarke • Music by James F. Hanley

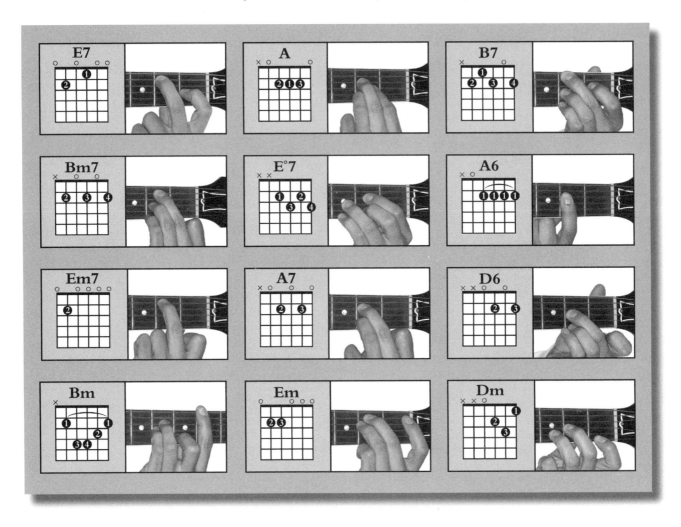

With spirit

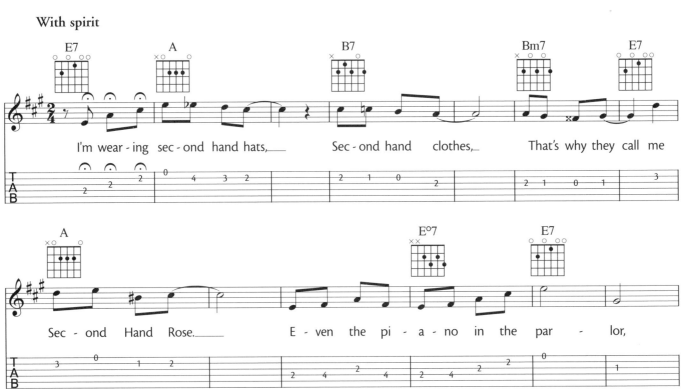

I'm wear-ing sec-ond hand hats,___ Sec-ond hand clothes,___ That's why they call me

Sec-ond Hand Rose.___ E-ven the pi-a-no in the par-lor,

SHE WORE A YELLOW RIBBON

American folk song

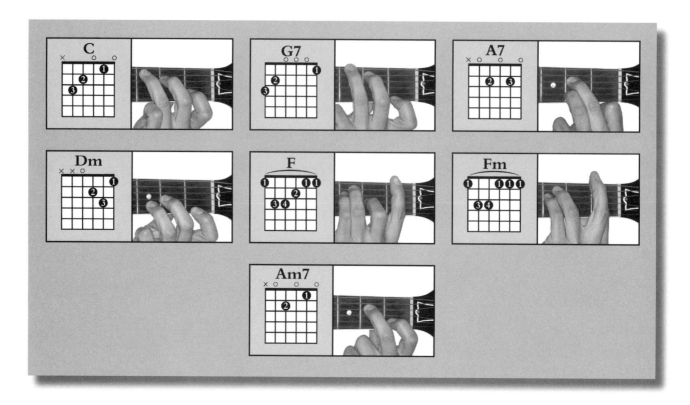

With spirit

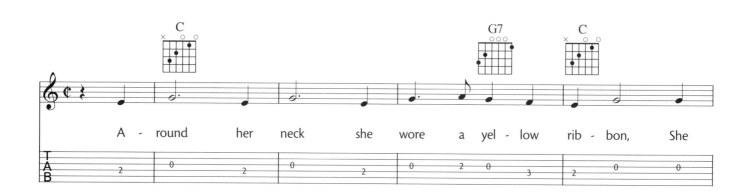

A - round her neck she wore a yel - low rib - bon, She

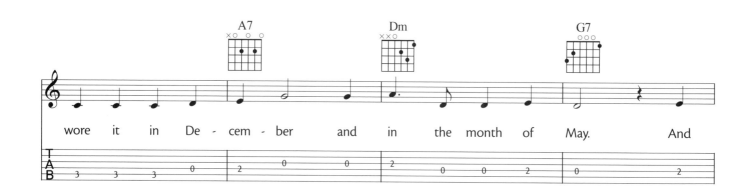

wore it in De - cem - ber and in the month of May. And

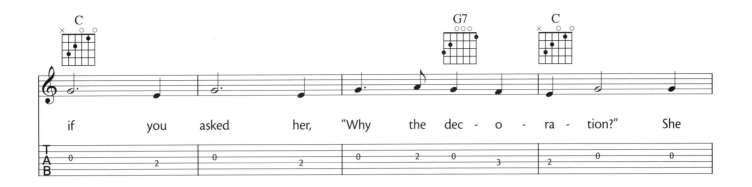

if you asked her, "Why the dec - o - ra - tion?" She

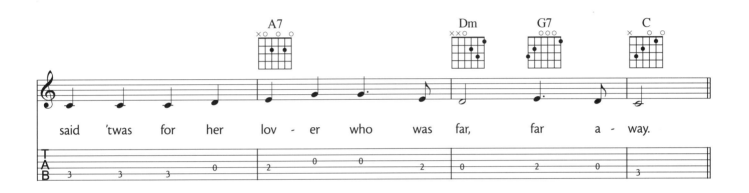

said 'twas for her lov - er who was far, far a - way.

Chorus

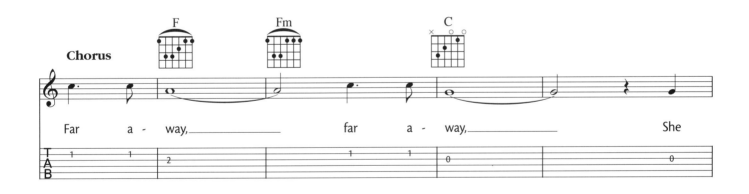

Far a - way,_____ far a - way,_____ She

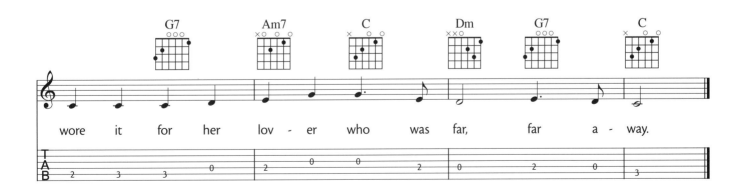

wore it for her lov - er who was far, far a - way.

SHENANDOAH

American folk song

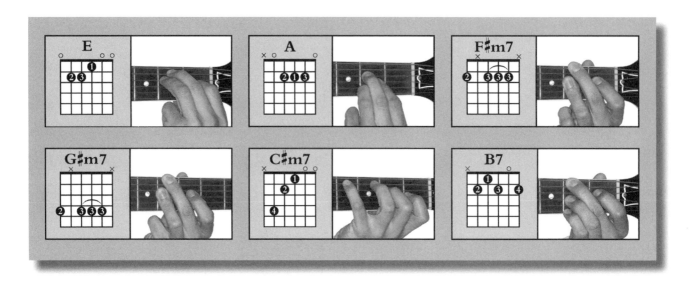

Freely

Oh, Shen-an doah,__ I long to hear you,__ A - way,____ you roll-ing riv-er, Oh,

Shen-an-doah,__ I long to hear you,__ A - way,____ I'm bound a -

way, 'Cross the wide_____ Mis-sour-ri.

2. Oh, Shenandoah, I love your daughter,
   Away, you rolling river,
   For her I'd cross your roaming water,
   Away, I'm bound away,
   'Cross the wide Missouri.

3. Oh, Shenandoah, I'm bound to leave you,
   Away, you rolling river,
   Oh, Shenandoah, I'll not deceive you,
   Away, I'm bound away,
   'Cross the wide Missouri.

SHINE ON HARVEST MOON

Words by Jack Norworth • Music by Nora Bayes & Jack Norworth

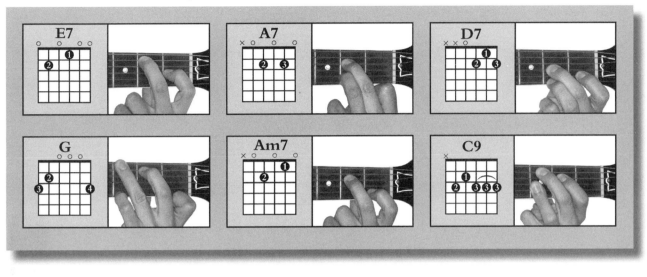

Moderately slow

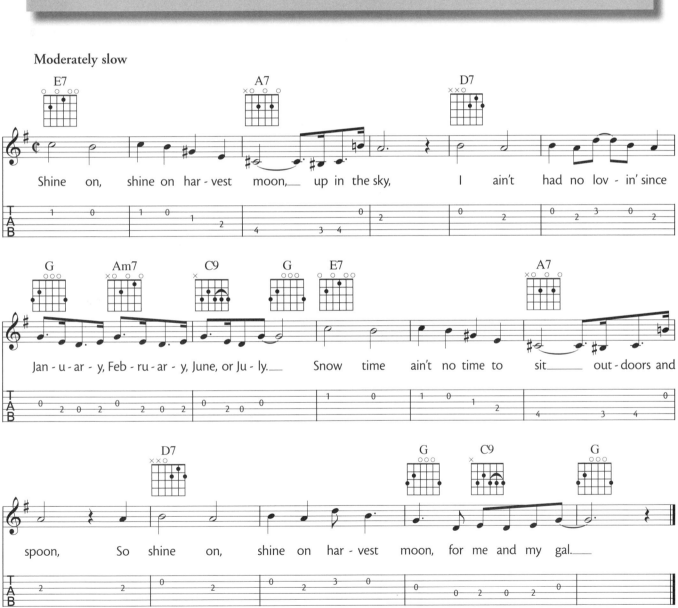

Shine on, shine on har-vest moon,___ up in the sky, I ain't had no lov-in' since

Jan-u-ar-y, Feb-ru-ar-y, June, or Ju-ly.___ Snow time ain't no time to sit___ out-doors and

spoon, So shine on, shine on har-vest moon, for me and my gal.___

THE SIDEWALKS OF NEW YORK

Words and music by Charles B. Lawlor & James W. Blake

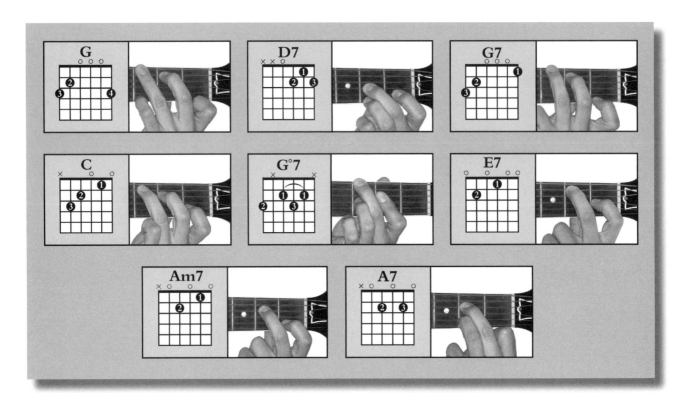

Moderately fast

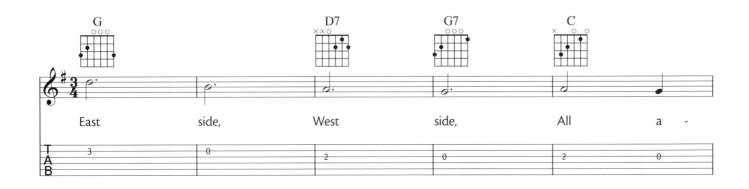

East   side,   West   side,   All   a -

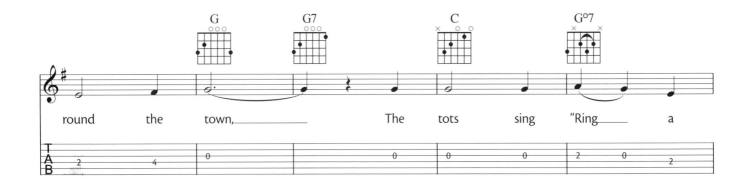

round   the   town,_____   The   tots   sing   "Ring_____   a

SIMPLE GIFTS

American folk song

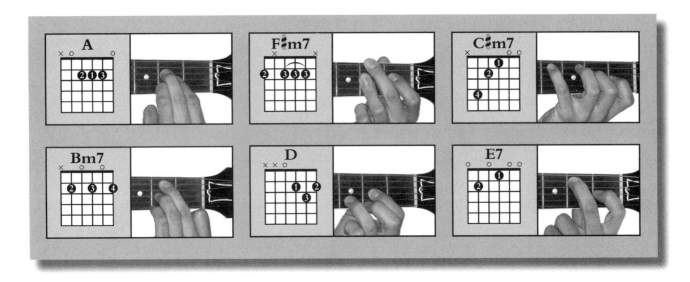

Moderately

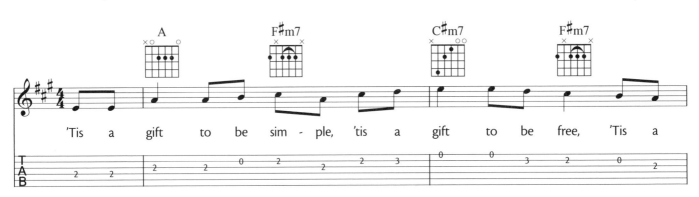

'Tis a gift to be sim - ple, 'tis a gift to be free, 'Tis a

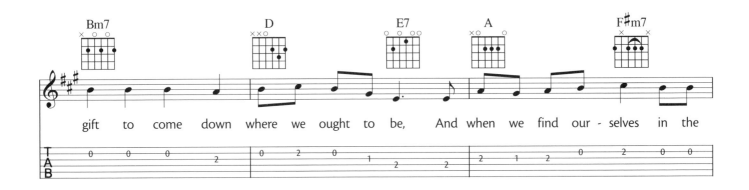

gift to come down where we ought to be, And when we find our - selves in the

SLOOP JOHN B.

West Indian folk song

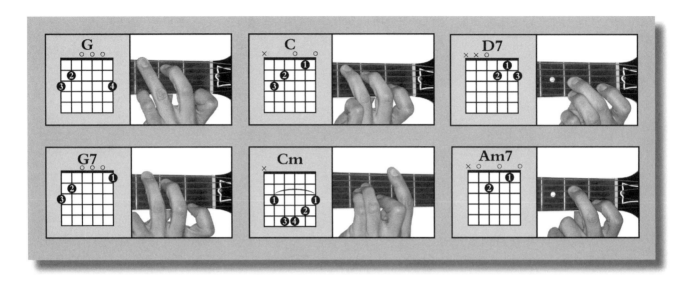

Moderately

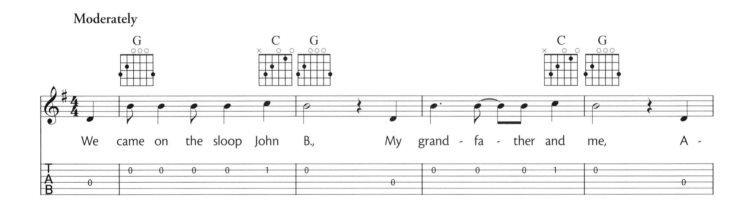

	G		C	G			C	G

We came on the sloop John B., My grand - fa - ther and me, A -

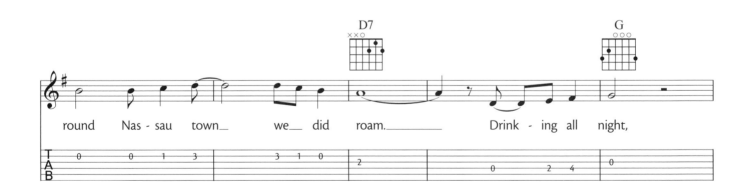

round Nas - sau town__ we__ did roam._____ Drink - ing all night,

SMILES

Words by Will Callahan • Music by Lee G. Roberts

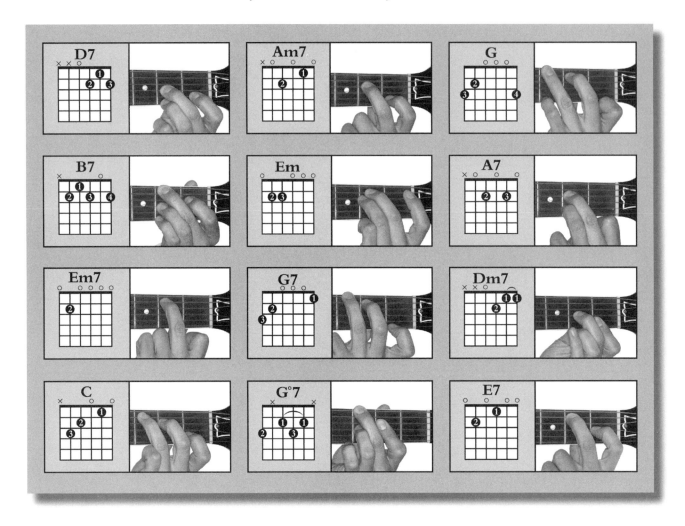

With movement

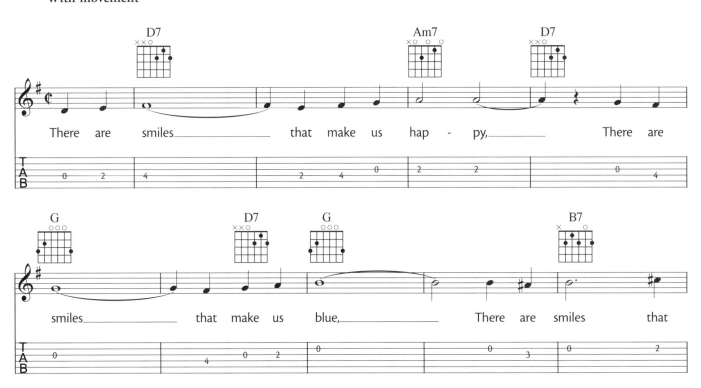

There are smiles_____ that make us hap - py,_____ There are

smiles_____ that make us blue,_____ There are smiles that

SOME OF THESE DAYS

Words and music by Shelton Brooks

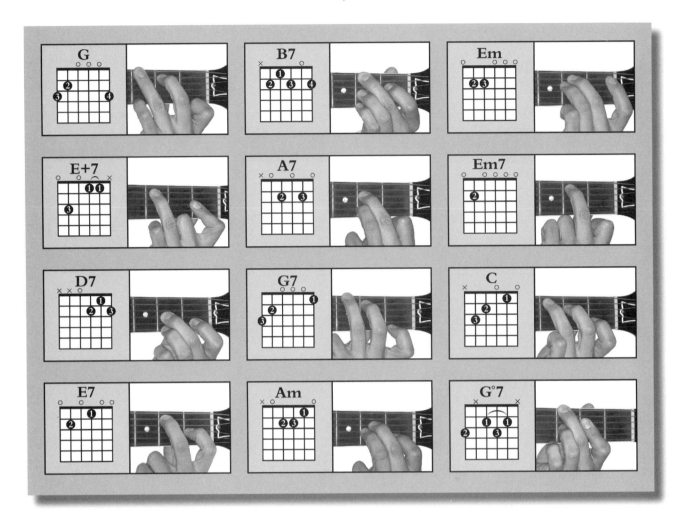

With movement

Some of these days___ You'll miss___ me hon - ey,___

___ Some of these days,___ You'll feel___ so lone - ly.___ You'll miss my hug - ging,

STAGOLEE

American folk song

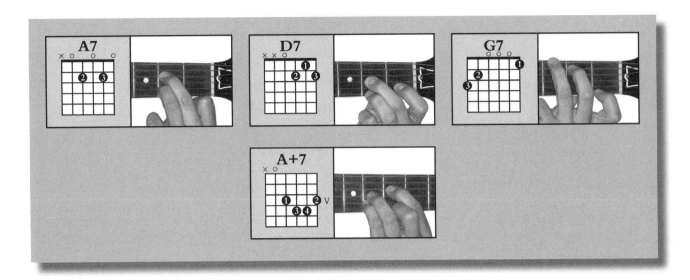

With a driving beat

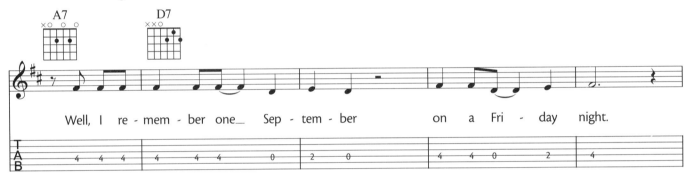

Well, I re-mem-ber one__ Sep-tem-ber on a Fri-day night.

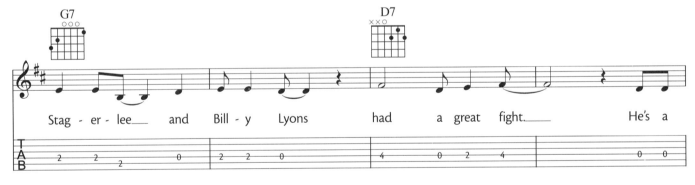

Stag-er-lee__ and Bill-y Lyons had a great fight.__ He's a

bad__ man,__ Oh, cru-el Stag-o-lee.__

2. Billy begged ole Stagolee, "Please don't take my life."
"I've got three children and a darling, loving wife."
He's a bad man
Oh cruel Stagolee.

3. Two o'clock next Tuesday, upon a scaffold high
People come from miles around just to watch ole
Stagolee die.
He's a bad man
Oh cruel Stagolee.

STEWBALL

American folk song

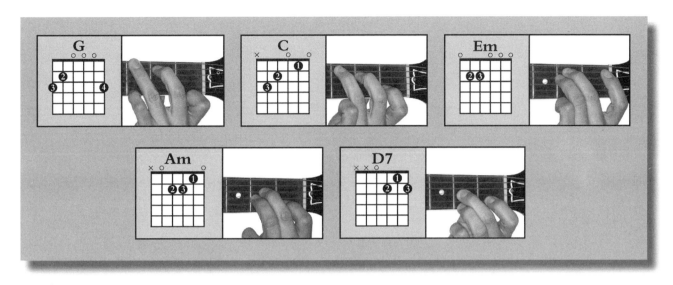

With movement

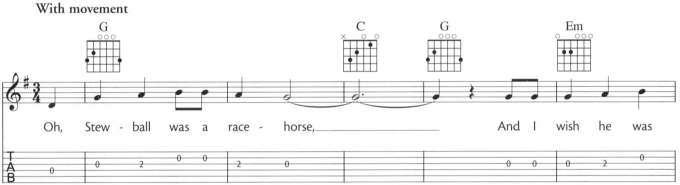

Oh, Stew - ball was a race - horse,_____ And I wish he was

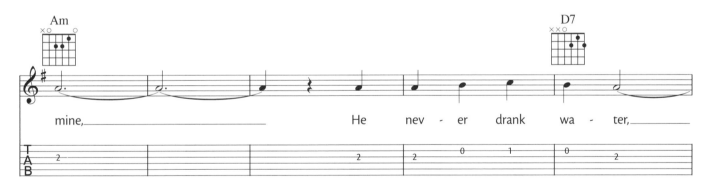

mine,_____ He nev - er drank wa - ter,_____

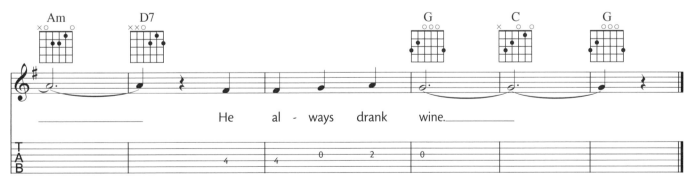

He al - ways drank wine._____

2. So come all of you gamblers,
   From near and from far,
   Don't bet your gold dollar
   On that little gray mare.

3. 'Cause way over yonder,
   Ahead of them all,
   Comes a-dancing and a-prancing,
   My noble Stewball.

THE STREETS OF LAREDO

American cowboy song

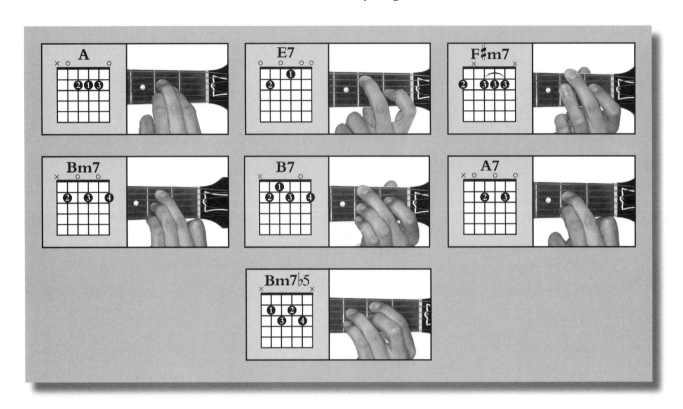

Moderately slow

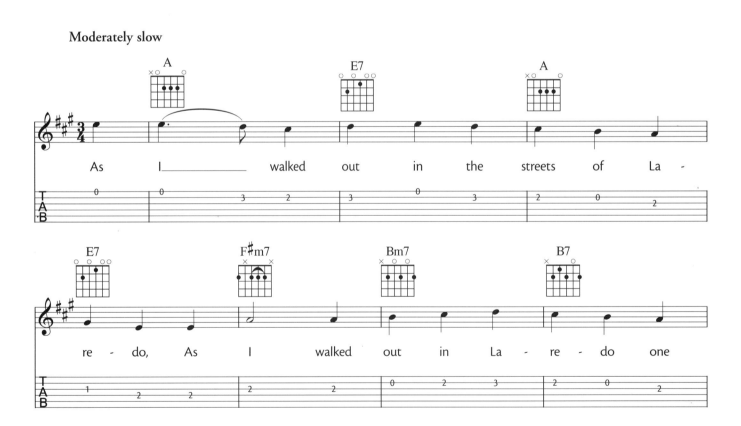

As I_____ walked out in the streets of La -

re - do, As I walked out in La - re - do one

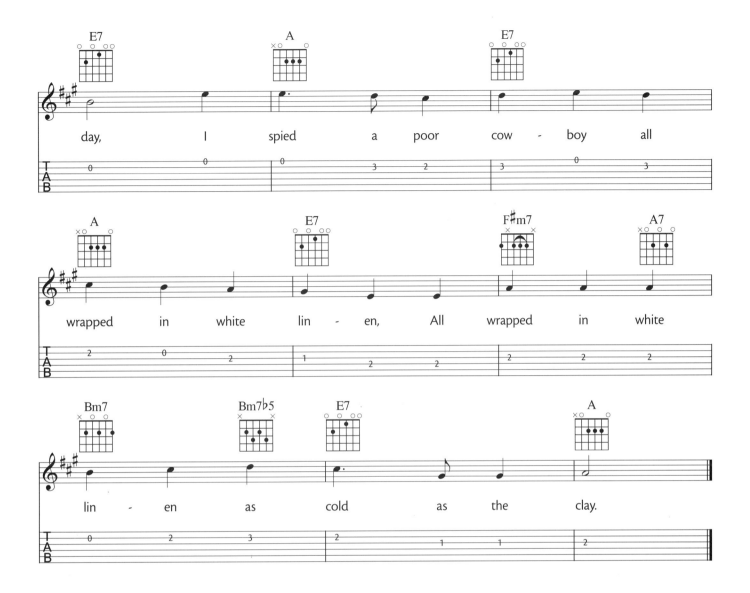

day, I spied a poor cow - boy all

wrapped in white lin - en, All wrapped in white

lin - en as cold as the clay.

2. "I see by your outfit that you are a cowboy,"
   These words he did say as I calmly went by,
   "Come sit down beside me and hear my sad story,
   I'm shot in the breast and I know I must die."

3. 'Twas once in the saddle I used to go dashing,
   With no one as quick on the trigger as I.
   I sat in a card game in back of the barroom,
   Got shot in the back and today I must die.

4. Get six of my buddies to carry my coffin,
   Six pretty maidens to sing a sad song.
   Take me to the valley and lay the sod o'er me,
   For I'm a young cowboy who knows he's done wrong.

5. "Oh, beat the drum slowly and play the fife lowly,
   And play the dead march as they carry my pall.
   Put bunches of roses all over my coffin,
   The roses will deaden the clods as they fall."

6. "Go fetch me a cup, just a cup of cold water,
   To cool my parched lips," the cowboy then said.
   Before I returned, his brave spirit had left him,
   And, gone to his Maker, the cowboy was dead.

7. We beat the drum slowly and played the fife lowly,
   And bitterly wept as we carried him along,
   We all loved our comrade, so brave, young, and
      handsome,
   We all loved our comrade although he done wrong.

STUMBLING

Words and music by Zez Confrey

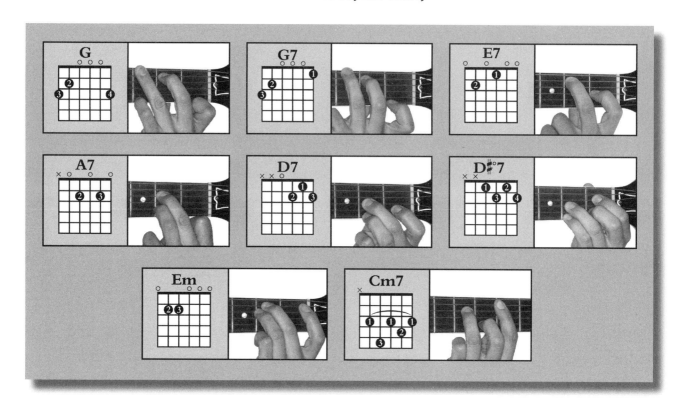

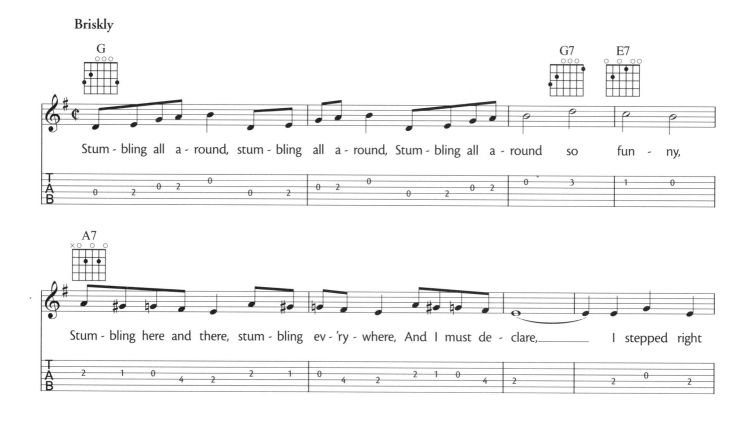

SWANEE

Words by Irving Caesar • Music by George Gershwin

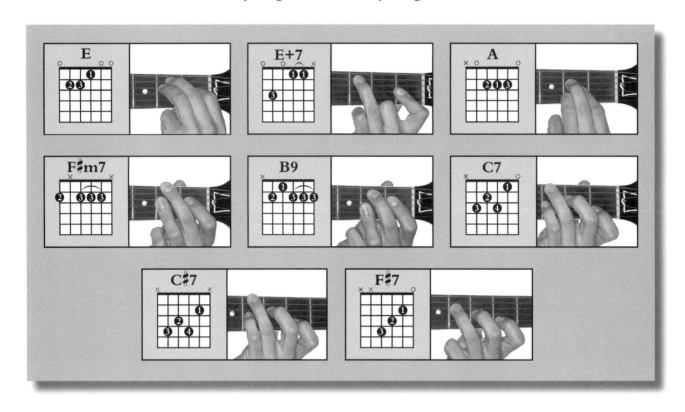

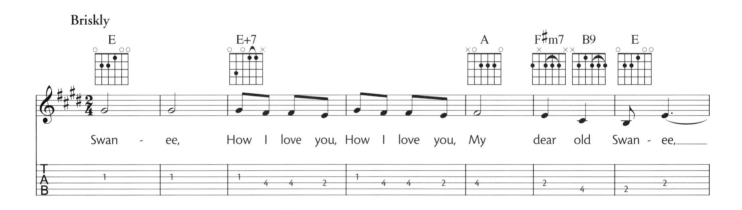

Swan - ee, How I love you, How I love you, My dear old Swan - ee,____

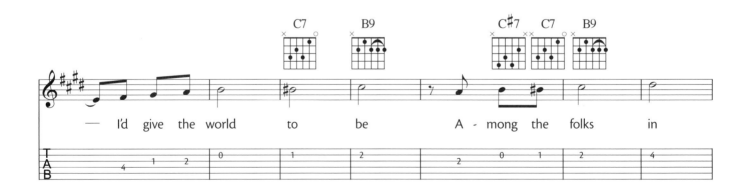

—— I'd give the world to be Among the folks in

TAKE ME OUT TO THE BALLGAME

Words by Jack Norworth • Music by Albert Von Tilzer

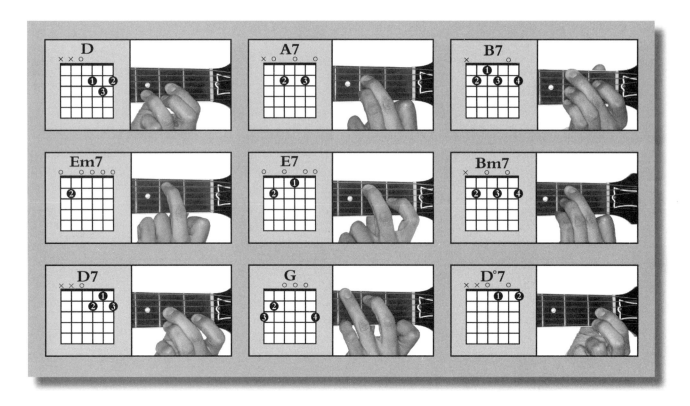

With spirit

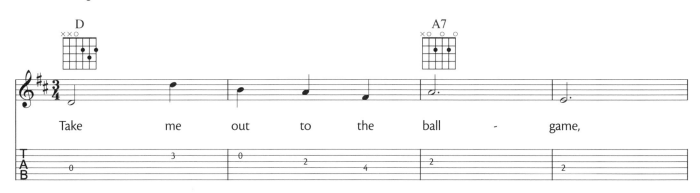

Take me out to the ball - game,

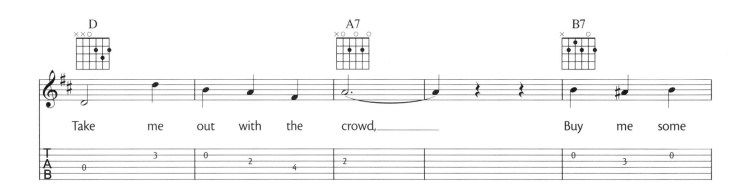

Take me out with the crowd,_____ Buy me some

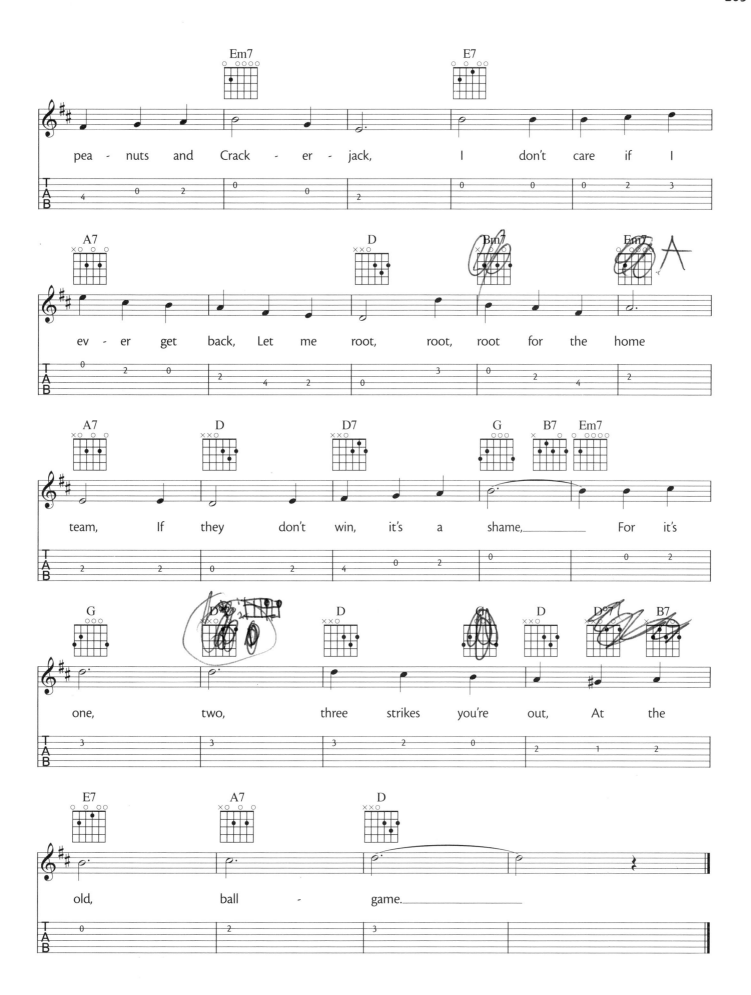

THEY DIDN'T BELIEVE ME

Words by Herbert Reynolds • Music by Jerome Kern

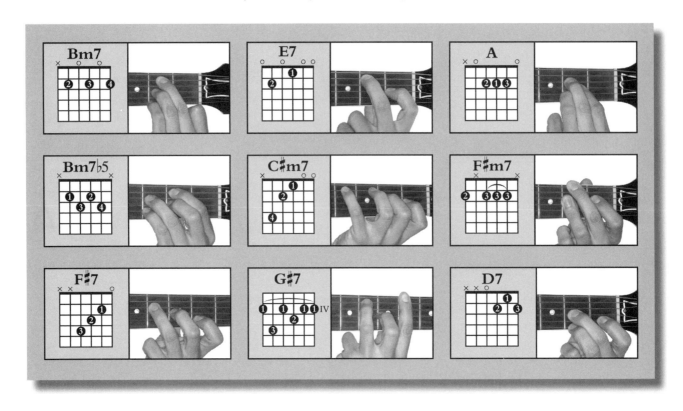

Moderately

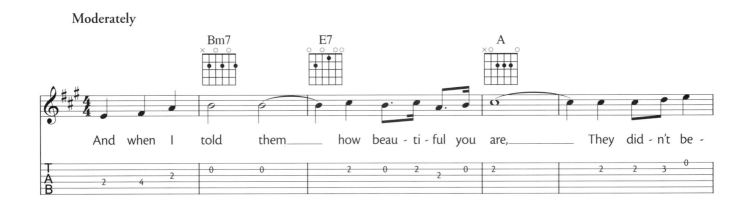

And when I told them____ how beau - ti - ful you are,____ They did - n't be -

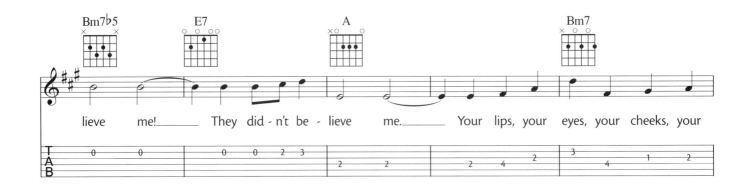

lieve me!____ They did - n't be - lieve me.____ Your lips, your eyes, your cheeks, your

THREE O'CLOCK IN THE MORNING

Words by Dorothy Terris (Theodora Morse) • Music by Julian Robeldo

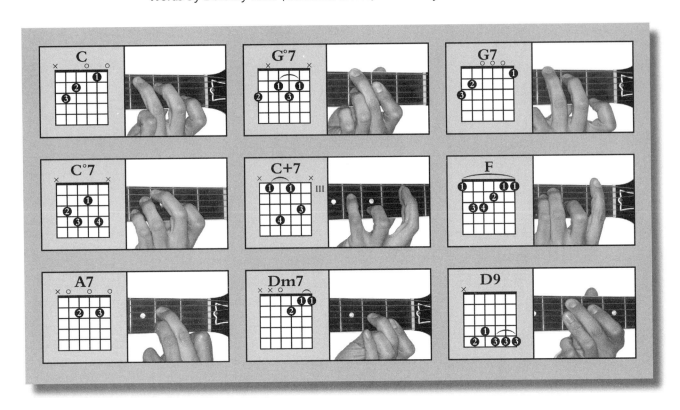

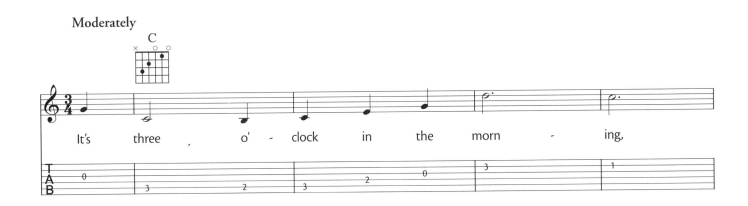

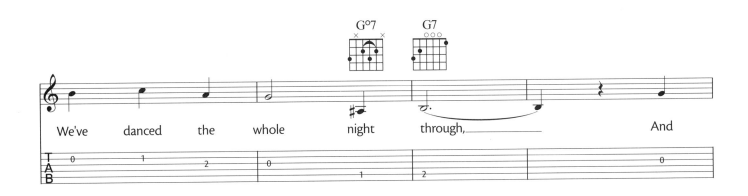

TOM DOOLEY

American folk song

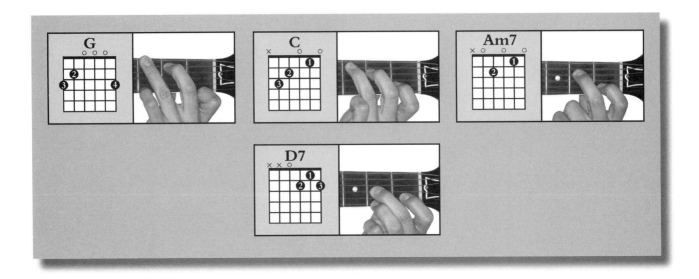

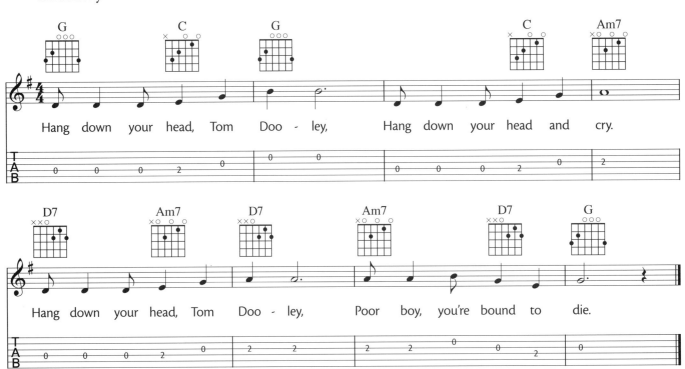

2. 'Round this time tomorrow,
   Wonder where he'll be?
   Down in some lonesome valley,
   Hangin' from the gallows tree.

3. Take my fiddle off the wall,
   Play it all you please,
   For at this time tomorrow,
   It'll be no use to me.

TOO-RA-LOO-RA-LOO-RAL

Words and music by James R. Shannon

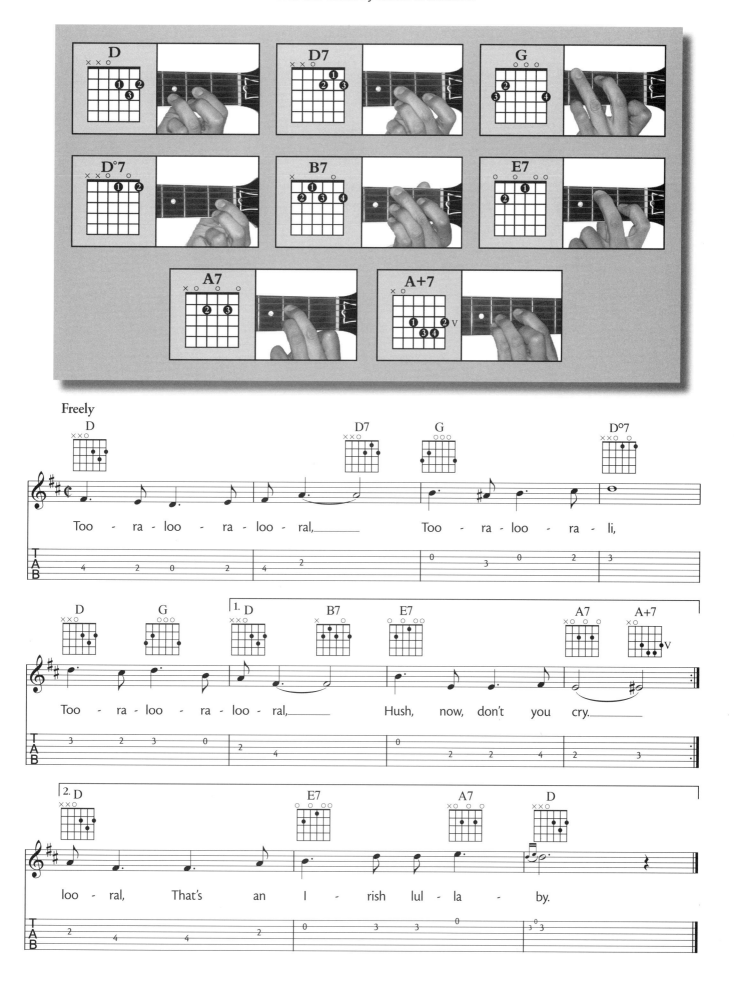

THE TRAIL OF THE LONESOME PINE

Words by Ballard MacDonald • Music by Harry Carroll

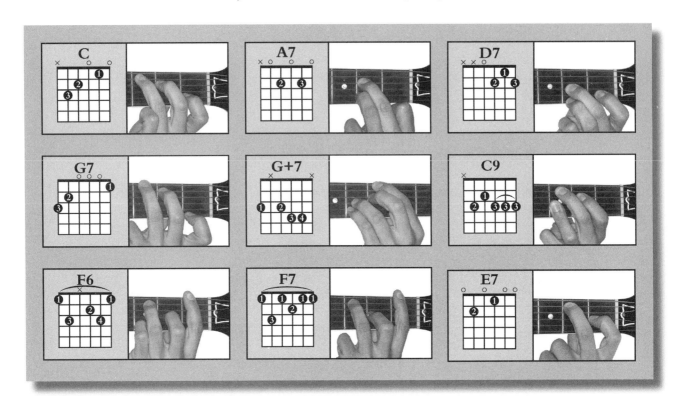

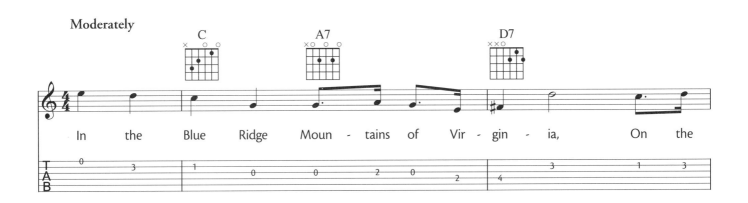

In the Blue Ridge Moun - tains of Vir - gin - ia, On the

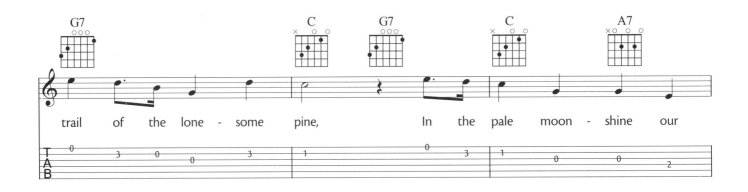

trail of the lone - some pine, In the pale moon - shine our

hearts en - twine, Where she carved her name and I carved mine. Oh,

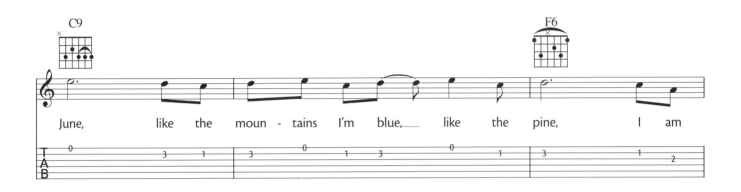

June, like the moun - tains I'm blue,___ like the pine, I am

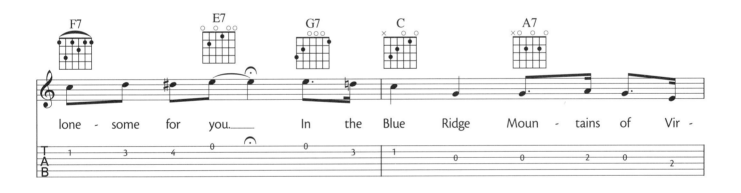

lone - some for you.___ In the Blue Ridge Moun - tains of Vir -

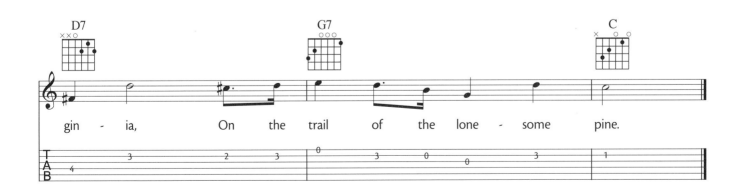

gin - ia, On the trail of the lone - some pine.

VIVE L'AMOUR

French folk song

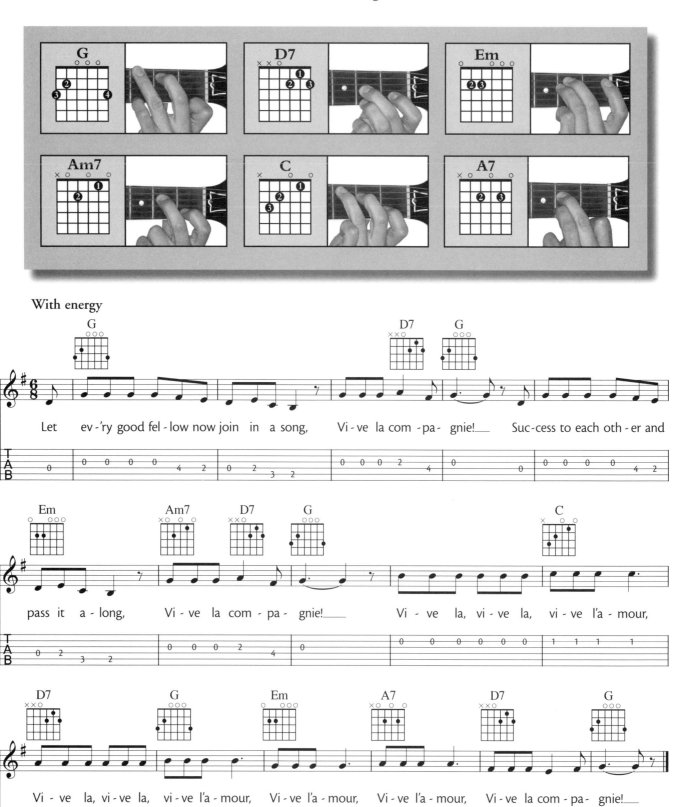

With energy

Let ev-'ry good fel-low now join in a song, Vi-ve la com-pa- gnie!___ Suc-cess to each oth- er and

pass it a-long, Vi-ve la com-pa- gnie!___ Vi-ve la, vi-ve la, vi-ve l'a-mour,

Vi-ve la, vi-ve la, vi-ve l'a-mour, Vi-ve l'a-mour, Vi-ve l'a-mour, Vi-ve la com-pa-gnie!___

THE WABASH CANNONBALL

American folk song

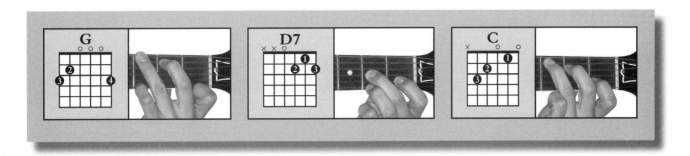

With energy

From the great At-lan-tic O-cean To the wide Pa-ci-fic's shore, From the ones we leave be-

hind us To the ones we see once more. She's might-y tall and hand-some, And

quite well known by all, She's a mod-ern com-bin-a-tion Called the Wa-bash Can-non-ball.

2. Hear the bell and whistle calling,
Hear the wheels that go "clack-clack,"
Hear the roaring of the engine,
As she rolls along the track.
The magic of the railroad
Wins hearts of one and all,
As we reach our destination
On the Wabash Cannonball.

3. Now the eastern states are dandies,
So the western people say
From New York to St. Louis
And Chicago by the way,
Through the hills of Minnesota
Where the rippling waters fall
No chances can be taken
On the Wabash Cannonball.

WAITING FOR THE ROBERT E. LEE

Words by L. Wolfe Gilbert • Music by Lewis F. Muir

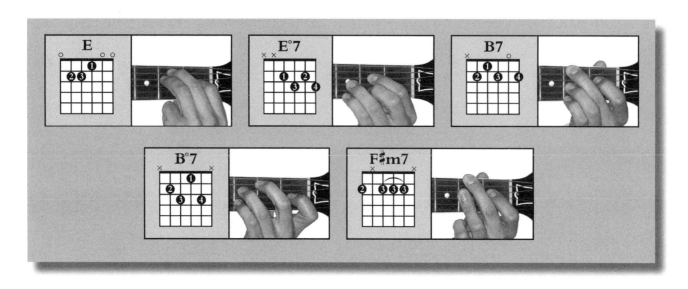

Moderately

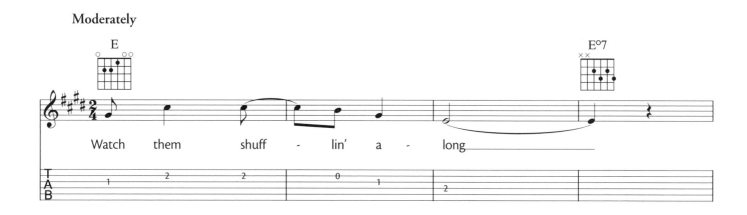

Watch them shuff - lin' a - long_____

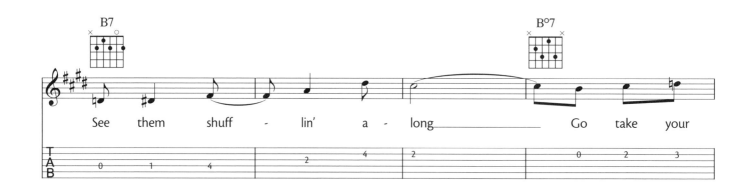

See them shuff - lin' a - long_____ Go take your

WALTZING MATILDA

Australian folk song

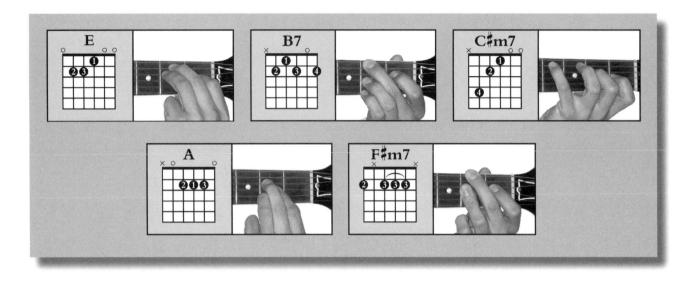

Moderately

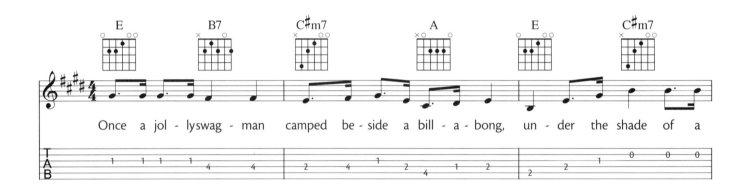

Once a jol-ly swag-man camped be-side a bill-a-bong, un-der the shade of a

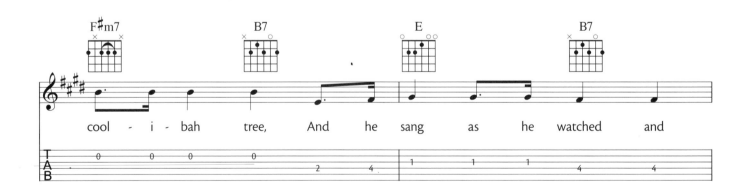

cool-i-bah tree, And he sang as he watched and

219

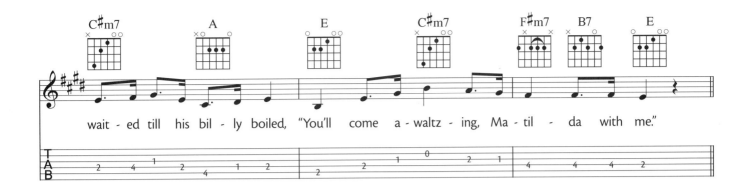

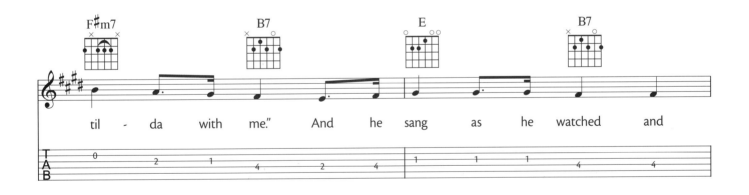

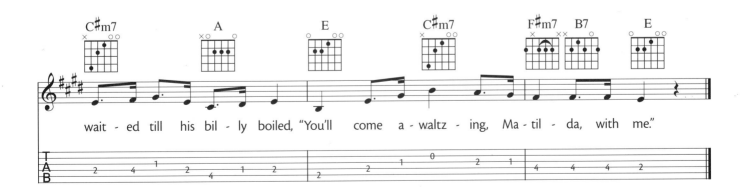

THE WATER IS WIDE

Welsh folk song

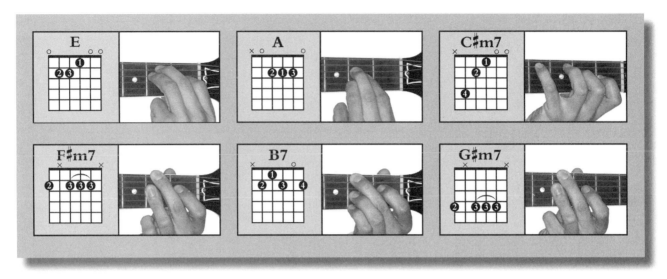

Sweetly

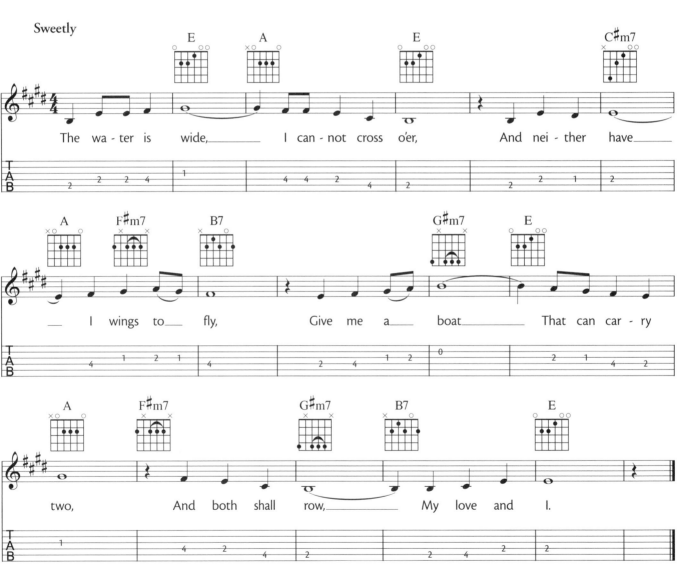

The wa-ter is wide,_____ I can-not cross o'er, And nei-ther have_____

_____ I wings to___ fly, Give me a___ boat_____ That can car-ry

two, And both shall row,_____ My love and I.

2.. Oh, love is gentle and love is kind,
The sweetest flow'r when first it's new,
But love grows old and waxes cold,
And fades away like the morning dew.

3. There is a ship and she sails the sea,
She's loaded deep as deep can be,
But not as deep as the love I'm in,
I know not if I sink or swim.

WE SHALL OVERCOME

American folk song

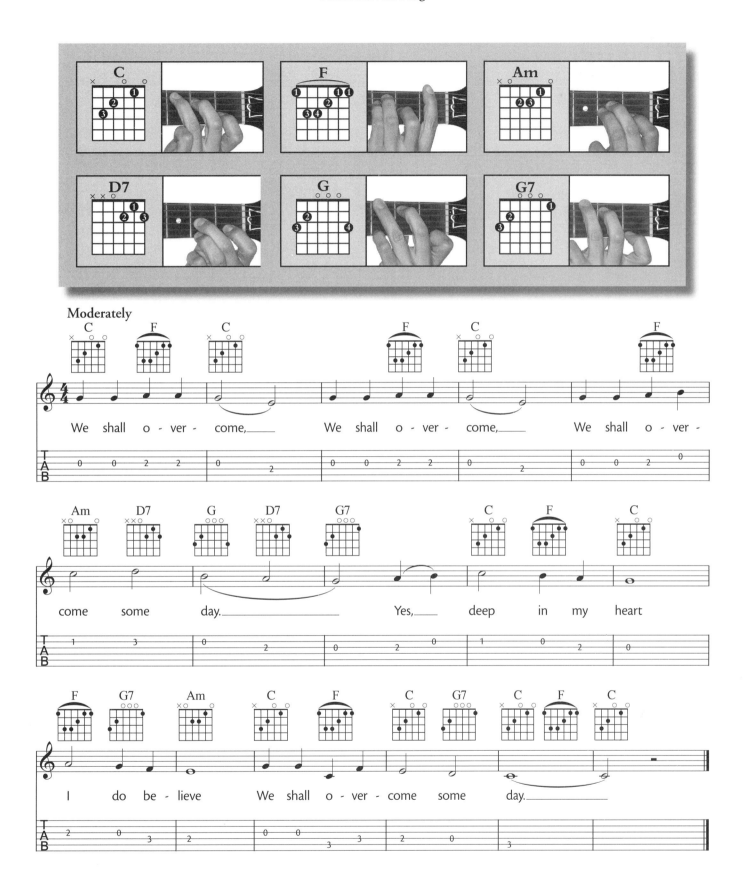

WAY DOWN YONDER IN NEW ORLEANS

Words and music by Henry Creamer & J. Turner Layton

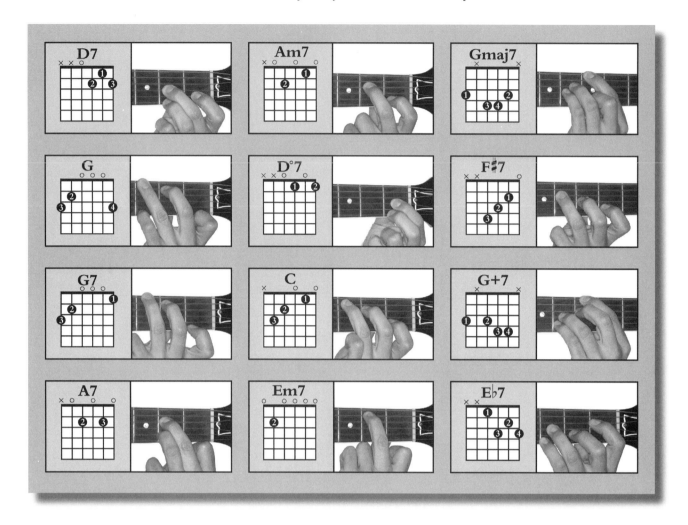

With movement

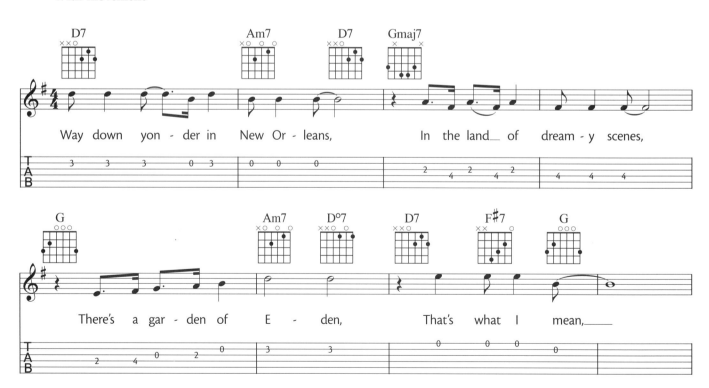

Way down yon-der in New Or-leans, In the land of dream-y scenes,

There's a gar-den of E - den, That's what I mean,

WHEN IRISH EYES ARE SMILING

Words by Chauncey Olcott & George Graff, Jr. • Music by Ernest R. Ball

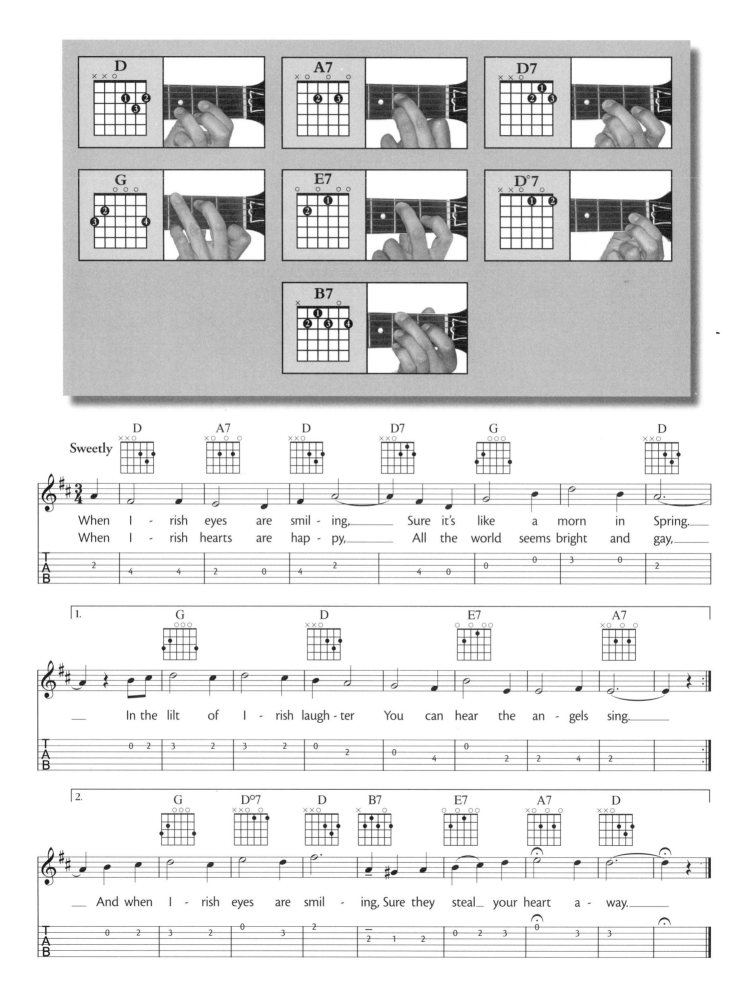

Sweetly

When I-rish eyes are smil-ing,_____ Sure it's like a morn in Spring.
When I-rish hearts are hap-py,_____ All the world seems bright and gay,_____

1.
_____ In the lilt of I-rish laugh-ter You can hear the an-gels sing._____

2.
_____ And when I-rish eyes are smil-ing, Sure they steal_ your heart a-way._____

WHEN THE SAINTS GO MARCHING IN

American spiritual

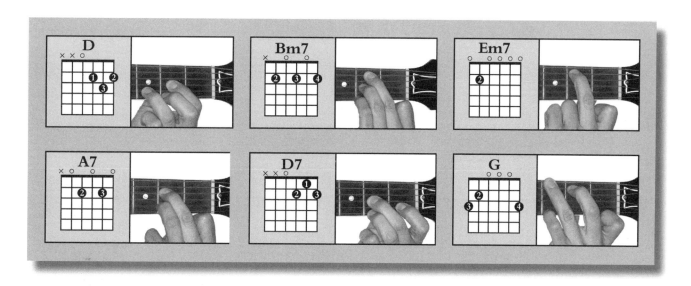

Moderately

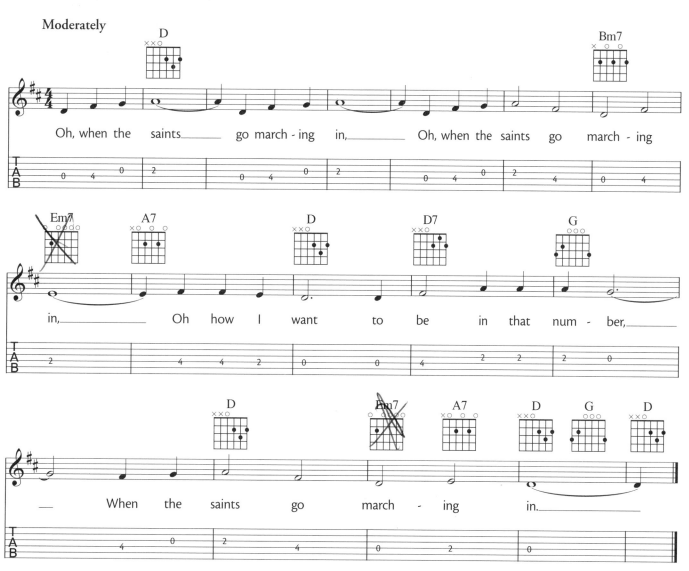

Oh, when the saints___ go march-ing in,___ Oh, when the saints go march-ing

in,___ Oh how I want to be in that num-ber,___

___ When the saints go march-ing in.___

2. Oh, when the sun refuse to shine,
Oh, when the sun refuse to shine,
How I want to be in that number,
When the sun refuse to shine.

3. I want to join the heav'nly band,
I want to join the heav'nly band,
I want to hear the trumpets blowing,
When the saints go marching in.

WHEN MY BABY SMILES AT ME

Words by Andrew B. Sterling & Ted Lewis • Music by Bill Munro

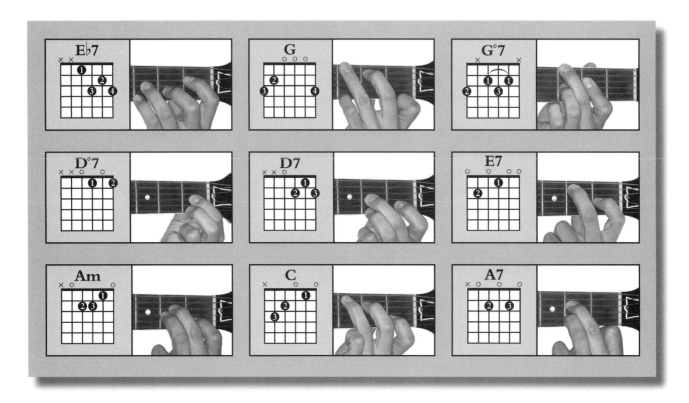

With movement

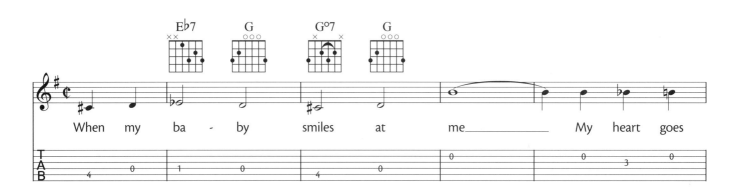

When my ba - by smiles at me_____ My heart goes

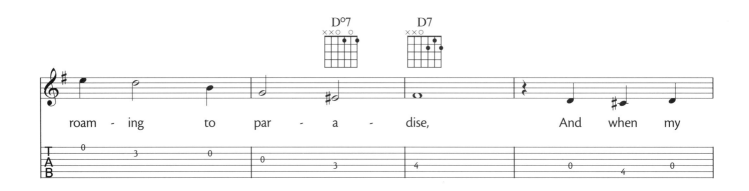

roam - ing to par - a - dise, And when my

WHILE STROLLING THROUGH THE PARK ONE DAY

Words and music by Ed Haley and Robert A. Keiser

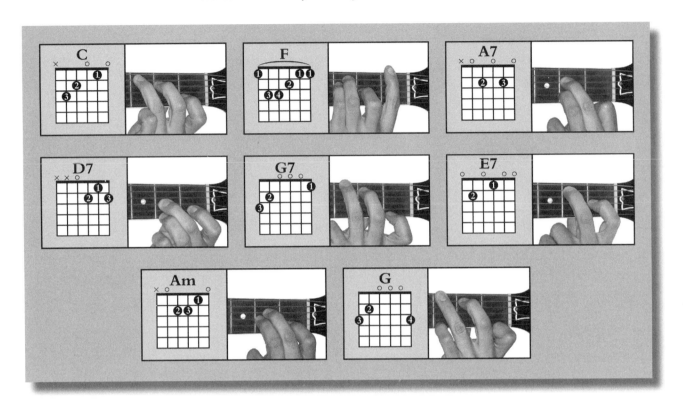

Moderately

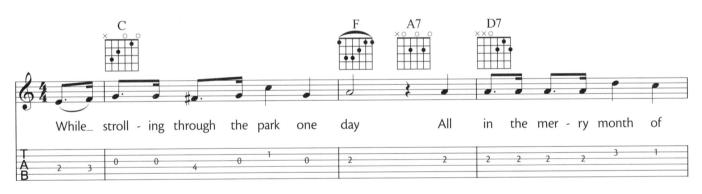

While_ stroll - ing through the park one day All in the mer - ry month of

May, I was tak - en by sur - prise by a pair of rogu - ish eyes, In a

WILD MOUNTAIN THYME

Scottish folk song

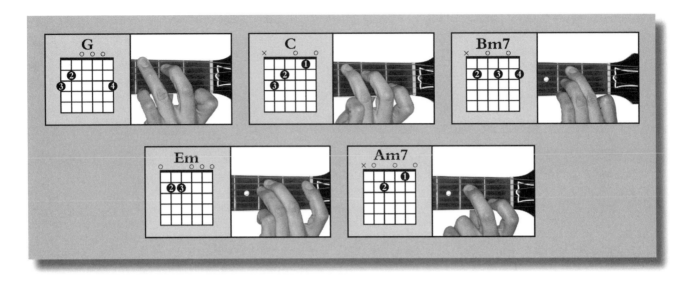

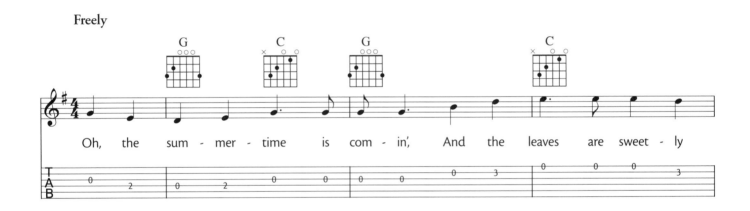

Freely

G	C	G		C

Oh, the sum - mer - time is com - in', And the leaves are sweet - ly

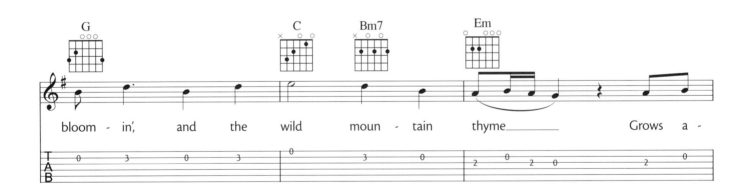

G	C	Bm7	Em

bloom - in', and the wild moun - tain thyme_____ Grows a -

2. I will build my love a tower
   By yon clear, crystal fountain,
   And on it I will twine
   All the flowers of the mountain.
   Will you go, laddie, go.
   Chorus

3. If my true love will not go,
   I will surely find another
   To pull wild mountain thyme,
   All around the purple heather.
   Will you go, lassie, go?
   Chorus

WIMOWEH

African folk song

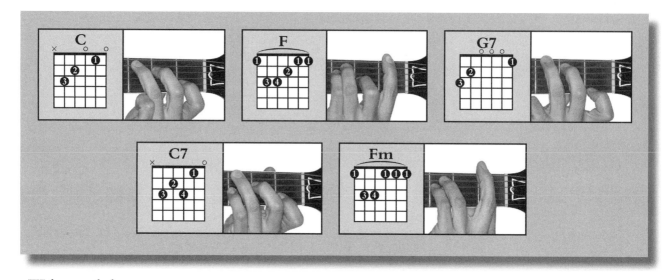

With a steady beat

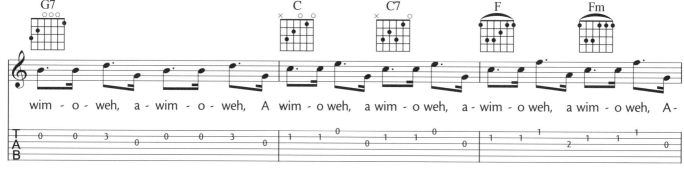

A - wim - o - weh, a - wim - o - weh, a - wim - o - weh, a - wim - o - weh, A - wim - o - weh, a - wim - o - weh, a -

wim - o - weh, a - wim - o - weh, A wim - o - weh, a wim - o - weh, a - wim - o - weh, a - wim - o - weh, A -

wim - o weh, a wim - o - weh, a - wim - o - weh, a - wim - o - weh, Wim - o - weh!

WORRIED MAN BLUES

American blues

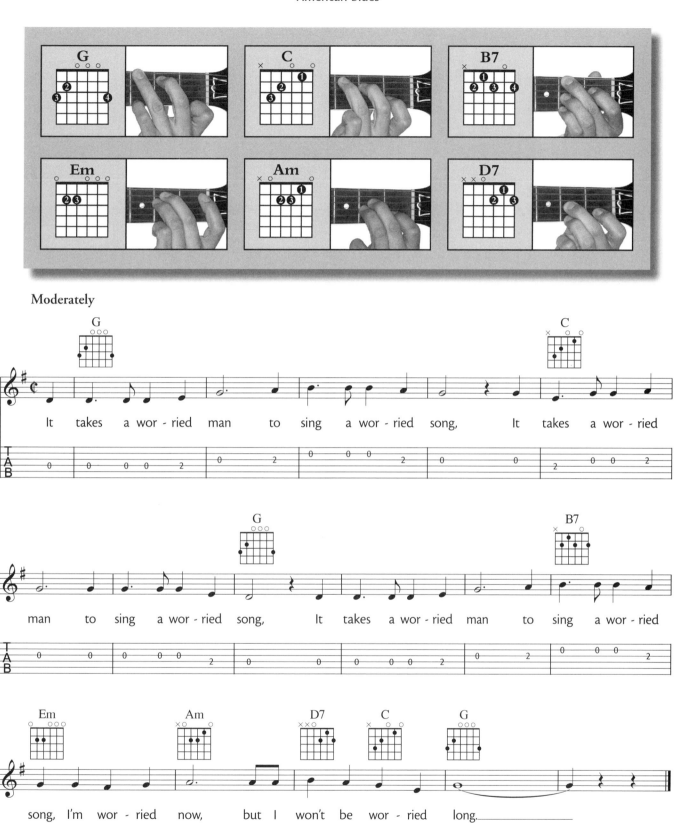

Moderately

It takes a wor - ried man to sing a wor - ried song, It takes a wor - ried

man to sing a wor - ried song, It takes a wor - ried man to sing a wor - ried

song, I'm wor - ried now, but I won't be wor - ried long.

THE YANKEE DOODLE BOY

Words and music by George M. Cohan

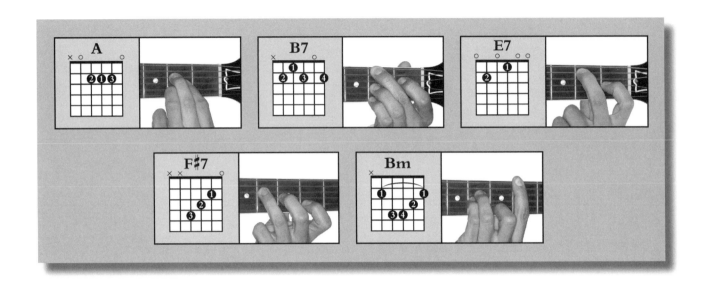

Sweetly

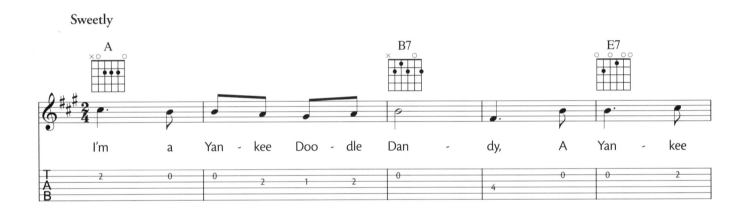

I'm a Yan - kee Doo - dle Dan - dy, A Yan - kee

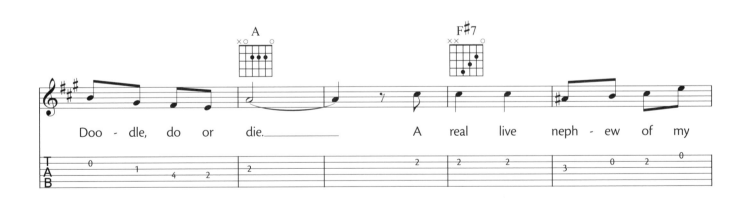

Doo - dle, do or die._____ A real live neph - ew of my

YOU MADE ME LOVE YOU

Words by Joseph McCarthy • Music by James V. Monaco

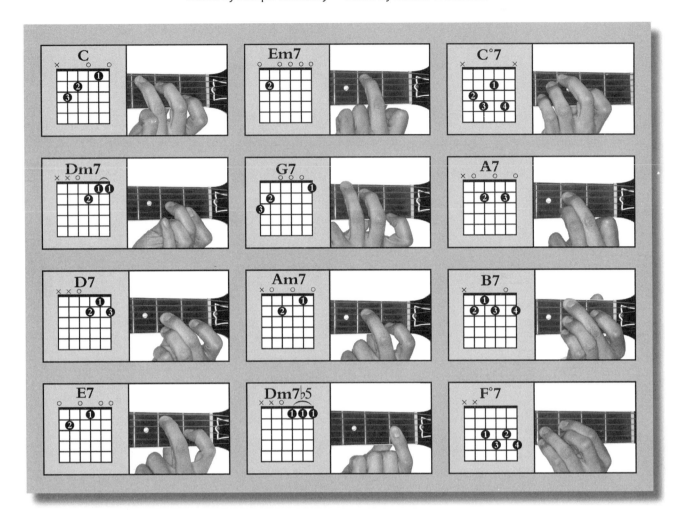

With movement

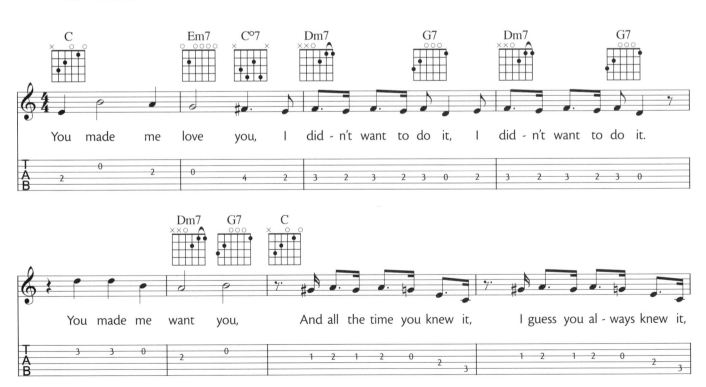

YOU'RE A GRAND OLD FLAG

Words and music by George M. Cohan

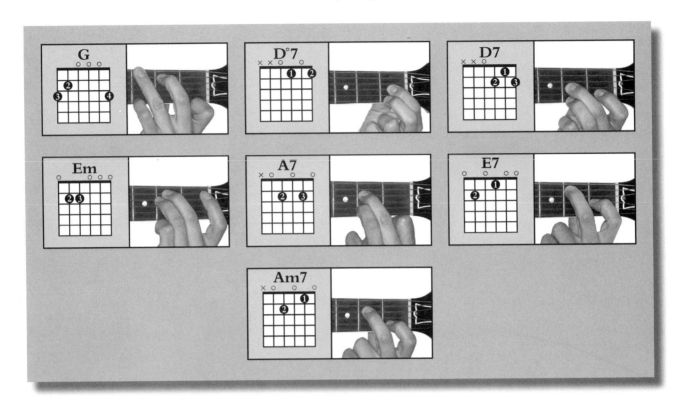

With energy

You're a grand, old flag, you're a high-fly-ing flag, And for-

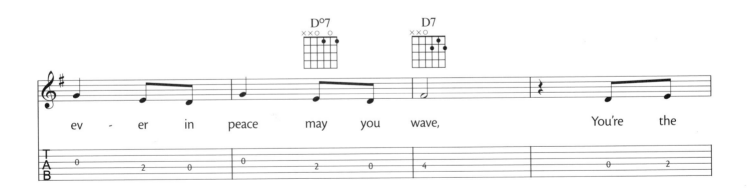

ev-er in peace may you wave, You're the